United States Department of the Treasury

Rules and Regulations Concerning Commerical Intercourse

with and in States and Parts of States Declared in Insurrection

United States Department of the Treasury

Rules and Regulations Concerning Commerical Intercourse
with and in States and Parts of States Declared in Insurrection

ISBN/EAN: 9783337876852

Printed in Europe, USA, Canada, Australia, Japan

Cover: Foto ©Suzi / pixelio.de

More available books at **www.hansebooks.com**

RULES AND REGULATIONS

CONCERNING

COMMERCIAL INTERCOURSE

WITH AND IN

STATES AND PARTS OF STATES DECLARED IN INSURRECTION,

THE COLLECTION, RECEIPT, AND DISPOSITION

OF

CAPTURED, ABANDONED, AND CONFISCABLE PROPERTY,

AND

THE EMPLOYMENT AND GENERAL WELFARE OF

FREEDMEN.

PRESCRIBED BY THE SECRETARY OF THE TREASURY, WITH THE APPROVAL OF THE PRESI-
DENT, IN PURSUANCE OF THE SEVERAL ACTS OF CONGRESS IN RELATION
TO THOSE SUBJECTS, AND APPENDED HERETO.

WASHINGTON:
JULY 29, 1864.

CONTENTS.

The following Regulations of the Secretary of the Treasury, having been seen and considered by me, are hereby approved : and commercial intercourse, in the cases and under the restrictions described and expressed in the Regulations, is licensed and authorized ; and all officers and privates of the regular and volunteer forces of the United States, and officers, sailors, and marines in the Naval service, will observe the said Regulations and the provisions of the several acts of Congress appended thereto, to which they relate, and will render all assistance not incompatible with military or naval operations, to officers and Agents of the Treasury Department executing the same.

ABRAHAM LINCOLN.

GENERAL REGULATIONS.

These Regulations, and the several Acts of Congress authorizing them, shall be executed and carried into effect, under direction of the Secretary of the Treasury, by the following officers:

A General Agent,
Supervising Special Agents,
Assistant Special Agents,
Local Special Agents,
Agency Aids,
Officers of the Customs designated by the Secretary, and
Superintendents of Freedmen.

All officers appointed under these Regulations are authorized to administer oaths required in the performance of their official duties.

The General Agent and the Supervising and Assistant Special Agents will be appointed by the Secretary of the Treasury; Local Special Agents and Agency Aids will be appointed by the Supervising Special Agents or Assistant Special Agents, as under Regulation XXVII, subject to the approval of the Secretary.

It shall be the duty of the General Agent, under the direction of the Secretary of the Treasury, to cause these Rules and Regulations to be properly and uniformly enforced in all States and parts of States declared in insurrection, and all Officers and Agents, appointed to perform duties under them, will comply with the instructions of the General Agent in regard thereto, until otherwise directed by the Secretary of the Treasury.

To facilitate the execution of the annexed Regulations, insurrectionary States and parts of States are hereby divided into districts called Special Agencies, distinguished numerically, and described as follows:

The *First* Special Agency comprises that part of the Valley of the Mississippi lying west of the Alleghany mountains and east of the mouth of the Tennessee river, and extending southwardly to include so much of the States of Alabama, Georgia, North Carolina, and Virginia as is, or shall be occupied by national forces operating from the North.

The *Second* Special Agency comprises so much of the Mississippi Valley as lies west of the mouth of the Tennessee river, including West Tennessee, the State of Arkansas, and so much of the States of Mississippi and Louisiana as is, or shall be occupied by national forces operating from the North.

The *Third* Special Agency comprises so much of the States of Louisiana, Mississippi, Alabama, and the west part of Florida, as is, or shall be occupied by national forces operating from the South.

The *Fourth* Special Agency comprises the State of Texas.

The *Fifth* Special Agency comprises the South and East part of Florida, including Key West, the State of South Carolina, and so much of the State of Georgia as is, or shall be occupied by national forces operating from the South.

The *Sixth* Special Agency comprises the State of North Carolina, excepting so much thereof as lies north of Albemarle Sound and east of Chowan river.

The *Seventh* Special Agency comprises that section of country lying east of the Alleghany mountains, and extending southwardly to include so much of the State of North Carolina as lies north of Albemarle Sound and east of Chowan river.

Additional Special Agencies, if established, will be numerically designated in the order of their establishment; and, if the boundaries of Agencies already established shall be changed, due notice thereof will be given.

Supervising Special Agents will supervise within their respective Agencies the execution of the Regulations, under the direction of the General Agent, and will make and, from time to time, change such Local Rules not inconsistent with them as may be proper for that purpose, and temporarily suspend or qualify the authority to grant permits for supplies, as the public interest shall require, subject to the approval of the General Agent, or of the Secretary of the Treasury: and they will confer with Generals commanding Departments, or, when such conference is impracticable, with Generals commanding Divisions or Districts, and with Naval officers commanding within the Agency under their supervision, and obtain, as far as practicable, their sanction to such action as may affect military or naval movements.

The Assistant and Local Special Agents, Agency Aids, and Officers of the Customs above referred to, will communicate directly with the Supervising Special Agent of the Agency to which they may be assigned upon all questions affecting the discharge of their duties under the Regulations. The several Supervising Special Agents will reply to these communications, except where they regard the intervention of the Department necessary, when they will transmit them, and all papers relating to them, with such recommendations as they may think proper, to the Secretary of the Treasury, and will keep the Department advised of their action in all matters pertaining to the execution of their duties.

W. P. FESSENDEN,
Secretary of the Treasury.

Dated Washington July 29th, 1864.

COMMERCIAL INTERCOURSE.

RULES AND REGULATIONS

UNDER THE SEVERAL ACTS OF CONGRESS PROHIBITING OR RESTRICTING COMMERCIAL INTERCOURSE WITH AND IN STATES AND PARTS OF STATES DECLARED TO BE IN INSURRECTION, AND IN PORTIONS OF LOYAL STATES IN DANGEROUS PROXIMITY THERETO.

PERMITS.

I. No goods, wares, or merchandise will be allowed to be transported to, from, or within any State or part of a State under restriction, or declared in insurrection, except under permits, certificates, and clearances, as hereinafter provided.

PERMIT OFFICERS.

II. The officers of the Treasury Department to be authorized under instructions from the Secretary to permit supplies to be transported to loyal persons residing in insurrectionary States or parts of States, or in restricted districts of loyal States with which commercial intercourse has been, or may be licensed by the President, under Regulations of the Secretary of the Treasury, are the Surveyors of Customs at Pittsburg, Wheeling, Cincinnati, Madison, Louisville, New Albany, Evansville, Paducah, Cairo, Quincy, St. Louis, Nashville, Memphis, and Baltimore; the Collectors of Customs at Boston, New York, Philadelphia, Georgetown, Alexandria, Beaufort in North Carolina, Port Royal in South Carolina, Brownsville, and New Orleans. Other officers will be designated to grant permits should the public interests require it; and the officers above named will respectively grant permits to such ports, places or districts only as shall be designated ·in the letter of instructions from the Secretary of the Treasury.

INTERCOURSE BEYOND MILITARY LINES PROHIBITED.

III. Commercial intercourse with localities beyond the lines of actual military occupation by the United States forces is absolutely prohibited; and no permit will be granted for the transportation of any property to any place under the control of insurgents against the United States.

LINES OF MILITARY OCCUPATION.

IV. Each Supervising Special Agent will ascertain from the pub lished order of the General commanding the Department or District embracing his agency, the lines of actual occupation by the military forces of the United States, and will confer with the Department commander, and agree with him in writing, as to the place or places, within those lines in his Agency, to which supplies may be taken for the loyal residents therein, and the aggregate amount which may be taken monthly to each of such places. Having so ascertained and agreed, he will promptly communicate the facts to the Secretary of the Treasury, and to the officers authorized to grant permits to the district so occupied.

SUPPLY STORES.

V. Supply stores at places agreed upon by the Commanding General of the Department and the proper Supervising Special Agent, may be established by such loyal persons as the Supervising Special Agent or Assistant Special Agents shall designate for that purpose. But the monthly amount agreed upon, as aforesaid, shall in no case be exceeded, and the maximum amount that any individual or firm may be permitted to take there for sale shall not exceed $3,000 per month, except in cities with a population over twenty thousand, and except in cases where the Commanding General of the district, for military reasons, requests it to be larger, in which cases all persons trading there shall be equally affected thereby, and no person shall be interested in more than one store.

APPLICATION FOR SUPPLY STORES.

VI. Any person desiring to establish a supply store at any place above provided, may make application in writing to the proper Supervising or Assistant Special Agent, who shall file the application, and record the name of each applicant with the date of application, in a book to be kept by him for that purpose; and all favoritism in granting the authorities so applied for shall be prevented as, far as possible, by Local Rules of the proper Supervising Special Agents. No application made prior to military occupation will be considered.

APPLICATION FOR AUTHORITY TO ESTABLISH A SUPPLY STORE.

...., 18.....

To ...., Special Agent, ... Agency:

Sir: ...., the undersigned, make application for authority to establish a Supply Store at ...., in the county of ...., and State of ...., under the regulations prescribed July 29, 1864, by the Secretary of the Treasury, concerning commercial intercourse with and in States declared in insurrection.

Respectfully, yours,

AFFIDAVIT OF APPLICANT FOR SUPPLY STORE.

Each applicant shall make and file with his application an affidavit in the following form:

" I....................................., of ...., in the county of ...., and State of......................., being duly sworn, on oath or affirmation say, that I am a citizen of the United States, (*native born or naturalized, as the case may be*,) and that I am in all respects true and loyal to the Government thereof; that I always have faithfully conformed and will, at all times, faithfully conform to the Proclamations and orders of the President of the United States, and the military Governors and Generals exercising authority under him, and to Departmental Regulations authorized by law ; and that I have aided and will, at all times, aid, by my conversation and conduct, and by every other means I can properly use in suppressing the rebellion, and restoring obedience to the Constitution and laws of the United States.

Subscribed and sworn before }
me this......day of ......, 18 . }

NO AUTHORITY GRANTED WITHOUT AFFIDAVIT.

VII. No authority to sell supplies, at any place in a State or part of State declared in insurrection, shall be given to any person who shall not accompany his application with the above affidavit taken before a competent officer.

AUTHORITY FOR SUPPLY STORE.

VIII. When authority shall be given to any person to establish a supply store at any place as above provided, it shall be in the following form :

...., of the county of ...., and State of ...., having applied to me for authority to establish a SUPPLY STORE at ...., in the county of ...., and State of ...., and having made and attached to .... application the prescribed affidavit, and executed a bond to the United States in a penalty and with sureties approved by me, I hereby authorize the said ....
to establish a SUPPLY STORE at ...., in the county of ...., and State of ...., and, under proper permits, to transport to and sell at said store, goods, wares, and merchandise, not prohibited, to an amount not exceeding .... dollars ($............) per month.

This authority is given subject to revocation at any time by the Supervising Special Agent of this Agency.

Dated at ...., this .... day of ...., 18....

BOND OF APPLICANT FOR SUPPLY STORE.

IX. Before the delivery of the authority above provided for, the applicant shall execute and deliver to the Agent a bond to the United States, in a penalty of twice the monthly amount authorized, with sureties to be approved by such Agent, which bond shall be in the following form :

Know all men by these presents, That we, ...,
of ...., as principal, and ....,
of ...., and .... of ....,
as sureties, are held and firmly bound unto the United States of America in the sum of .... dollars, ($..............,) to be paid to the United States of America ; for which payment, well and truly to be made, we bind ourselves, our heirs, executors, and administrators, jointly and severally, firmly by these presents. Sealed with our seals, and dated this .... day of ...., in the year one thousand eight hundred and ....

Whereas, the said .... has applied for and received authority to establish a SUPPLY STORE at ...., in the county of ...., and State of ...., under the license of the President and the regulations prescribed by the Secretary of the Treasury, July 29, 1864.

The condition of the above obligation is such, That if the said ....
.... shall not transport goods to any place other than such SUPPLY STORE, nor engage, directly or indirectly, in any prohibited trade ; and if no part of the goods transported by .... shall, with .... knowledge or assent, or by .... connivance, be so used or disposed of as to give aid or encouragement to the insurgents ; and if no military, naval, or civil officer, or person prohibited by law from trading, or receiving, or expecting profit or advantage from trade in an insurrectionary State, shall be interested, directly or indirectly, in any sale made from said store ; and if no goods, wares, or merchandise are sold or disposed of at said store, or other act done by him, or by others acting under his authority, in violation of any regulation of the Secretary of the Treasury, or local rule of the Supervising Special Agent, then the above obligation to be void, otherwise to remain in full force and effect.

Signed, sealed, and delivered ⎱
    in presence of--   ⎰
          —— ——, [L. S.]
          —— ——, [L. S.]
          —— ——, [L. S.]

RECORDS OF AUTHORITIES.

X. Records shall be kept in the office of each Supervising and District Agency, in which every authority granted therein shall be recorded, with the locality of the supply store, the name of the party authorized, and his sureties with their respective residences, the date and monthly amount of the authority, and the date and amount of each shipment of goods authorized. And whenever a party authorized to sell, as aforesaid, shall desire to transport supplies to his store, he shall file, with the Supervising or Assistant Special Agent, in charge of the record of his authority, an application for such supplies, with a full memorandum thereof. Whereupon such agent may, if he knows no reason why he should not, give the applicant a certificate in the following form :

CERTIFICATE FOR SUPPLIES.

This certifies that...................................... is duly authorized to sell supplies to loyal persons at ...., and that he may be permitted to ship to that place, during the month of ...., supplies included in the annexed memorandum to the amount of $......................

The Permit Officer to whom this certificate is presented, if the party holding it desires to ship only a part of the amount named therein, will indorse upon the certificate the date and amount of the permit, and will give the holder a certified copy of the original certificate with his indorsement thereon, retaining the original as his authority for the permit.

And the officer granting a permit on the certified copy will, in like manner, indorse upon it the date and amount of his permit, and give a certified copy of the certificate and indorsements as certified, and so on until the amount of the original certificate is exhausted ; so that the stock permitted to, and transported by the trader, each month, shall not exceed the amount above named. No permit will be granted upon this certificate after the close of the month of .... , 18......

Dated at ...., this .... day of ...., 18 .....
         ...., *Special Agent.*

To which certificate he shall annex a copy of the memorandum so filed with him, countersigned with his approval.

PERMIT FOR SUPPLY STORE.

XI. Upon presentation of the above certificate, or the certified copies thereof as provided, together with the application, copies, invoices, and affidavits, as hereinafter named, any permit officer named in regulation II may permit the shipment of supplies included in the memorandum annexed to the certificate, so that the aggregate amount of the shipments under the certificate shall not exceed the sum named therein. Such permit shall be made subject to the approval of the permit officer of the last port of shipment in a loyal State through which the supplies shall pass *en route* to their destination.

XII. The application for permit shall be in the following form:

APPLICATION FOR PERMIT FOR SUPPLIES.

To ....

Sir: .... desire permission to transport from this port to .... the supplies named in the invoices of which the annexed are true copies, which supplies were purchased by .... of the parties respectively indicated by the invoices, and are owned by .... of ...., and consigned to .... of ...., and are contained in .... packages, which packages are marked and described as follows:

No. of Packages.	Marks.	Description of Supplies.	Value.

AFFIDAVIT OF APPLICANT FOR PERMIT FOR SUPPLIES.

XIII. The original invoices shall be presented with the application, and shall be compared with the copies annexed thereto by the officer granting the permit to ship. The applicant shall annex and file, with his application for permit to ship, an affidavit in the following form:

...., of ...., being duly sworn deposes and says that .... is the owner of the goods, wares, and merchandise described in the invoices, true copies of which are hereto attached, and that the quantities, descriptions, and values of the said goods, wares, and merchandise are correctly stated in said invoices; that the marks on the packages are correctly stated in the above application; and that the packages contain nothing except as stated in the invoices.

And this deponent further swears, that the goods, wares, and merchandise permitted to be transported upon the above application, shall not, nor shall any part thereof, be transported or disposed of by him, or by his authority, connivance, or assent, in violation of the terms of the permit.

PERMIT FOR SUPPLIES.

XIV. If the permit officer is satisfied that no fraud has been, or is being practiced, he may permit the shipment so applied for, in the following form:

PORT OF ....

This may certify, That .... has this day filed in my office an application for permit to transport from this port to ...., to be delivered to .... at ...., by way of.......................... the goods, wares, and merchandise mentioned and described in the copies of invoices thereof hereto attached, (each one of which is stamped with my official seal,) which are contained in .... packages, and are of the aggregate value of $ ...., and are owned by ...., shipped by ...., consigned to ....

And the said .... has presented with his application the original invoices of the said goods, wares, and merchandise, and filed in my office copies thereof, and made oath before me pursuant to the regulations of the Secretary of the Treasury, and local rules made under then:

Now, THEREFORE, by virtue of the authority of the President of the United States, conferred on me through the Secretary of the Treasury, I do hereby authorize and permit the said .... to transport, by the route above named, the said goods, wares, and merchandise to . ...

The right is reserved to revoke, suspend, or qualify this permit, at such time and place and in such manner as the public interests may require; and it will expire ten days after date, and cease to have any force, except that merchandise properly shipped under it, within ten days, will be allowed to go to its place of destination.

In testimony whereof I hereunto set my hand and affix }
the seal of this office, this .... day of ...., }
one thousand eight hundred and sixty .... }

—————— ——————,
.... of Customs.

To which permit the officer granting the same shall annex copies of the invoices presented, with the application, except that the extension of prices need not be made in the copies annexed to the permit to transport, but the value of each lot shall be stated in the original invoices.

ACCOUNTS OF SALES OF SUPPLIES.

XV. All persons authorized to sell supplies shall keep true accounts of all their sales, with the name and residence of each purchaser, and the date and amount of each sale: and their books, invoices, and accounts, shall at all times be open to the inspection of the Supervising or Assistant Special Agents. If any person so authorized shall violate any Regulation or local rule, his authority shall be immediately revoked, and his stock in trade shall be seized and forfeited to the United States, and such steps shall be promptly taken as may be necessary to secure its condemnation by a court of competent jurisdiction.

NO SALES EXCEPT BY PERSONS AUTHORIZED.

XVI. No goods, wares, or merchandise shall be sold at any place in a State declared in insurrection, except by persons duly authorized, and none shall be transported from any place at which supplies are authorized to be sold, except under the permit of the Local Special Agent appointed for that place. Loyal persons residing in the district of country contiguous to the place, and within the lines of actual occupation by the military forces of the United States as indicated by published order of the Commanding General of the Department or District in which it is situated, may be permitted by the Local Special Agent to procure from any such store and take to their homes such individual, family, or plantation supplies as may be necessary for their own use, as provided in Regulation XVIII.

FAMILY SUPPLIES.

XVIII. The permit above provided for shall be given by the Local Special Agent, upon application of the head of the family, or some person duly authorized by him or her in writing, and then only on an affidavit in the following form:

AFFIDAVIT OF APPLICANT.

State of .... }
County of .... } *ss.*

           I...........................being duly sworn, depose and say that.........reside at .... in the County of .... and State of .... and that .... has resided there for .... years last past: that I am in all respects true and loyal to the Government of the United States, and that I will in all things so deport myself, bearing true faith and allegiance thereto, and to the best of my ability protecting and defending the same. That .... family consists of .... white and .... colored persons : that the supplies, invoices of which are hereto attached, are necessary for the use and consumption of said family during the ensuing month : that no part thereof shall be sold or otherwise disposed of by .... or by .... authority, connivance, or consent, except for the sole use and consumption of said family; and that, to the best of my knowledge and belief, no application has been made for any permit for the same or like supplies, to any other officer or agent, and that no supplies for the same family, for the period mentioned, have been or are expected to be applied for elsewhere, or otherwise obtained.

    Subscribed and sworn before me }
this .... day of............... 186 }

PERMIT FOR FAMILY AND PLANTATION SUPPLIES.

XVIII. If the Local Special Agent is satisfied as to the truth of the affidavit and the good faith of the applicant, he shall permit the purchase and transportation applied for, subject to the approval of the Commander of the Post, or such person as he shall designate for that purpose, to be countersigned upon the permit, which permit shall be in the following form:

    This may certify that .... has this day filed in my office an

2

application and the required affidavit for purchase of the .... supplies described in the annexed memorandum countersigned by me, the aggregate value whereof is $.................., and for transportation thereof by way of .... to the place of residence of ....

And by virtue of the authority vested in me, I do hereby permit the said .... to purchase the said supplies at ...., and to transport them from .... to ....

This permit will expire and cease to have any force ten days after its date.

....

Local Special Agent,

.... *Special Agency.*

DATED at ...., }
this .... day of ...., 18 . }

CERTIFICATE TO PURCHASE ELSEWHERE.

XIX. If the applicant prefers to purchase the supplies at some place in a loyal State, then, instead of the above permit he shall give him a certificate in the following form:

I certify that .... has made the prescribed affidavit and application before me for the supplies, a memorandum whereof is hereto attached, and countersigned by me, the estimated value whereof is $........., which he desires to take to his home in the County of ...., State of ....

I hereby recommend any authorized permit officer, to permit the transportation of said supplies, to an amount not exceeding $........., from the port where it is applied for to his home aforesaid, upon presentation of this certificate, countersigned with the approval of the General commanding this post, or some person authorized by him.

This certificate will cease to have any force thirty days after date.

Dated at ...., this .... day of ...., 186...

———— ————,

Local Special Agent.

PERMIT FOR TRANSPORTATION.

XX. Upon presentation of this certificate so countersigned, with duplicate invoices of the supplies to be transported, any authorized permit officer may grant the permit desired, in the following form:

In compliance with the recommendation of ...., Local Special Agent at ...., approved by the proper military officer, permission is hereby granted to ...., residing at .... , in the County of ...., and State of .... , to take from this port to his home aforesaid, the supplies mentioned in the invoices hereto attached and countersigned by me.

Dated at ...., this .... day of ...., 186...

CERTIFICATE TO BE FILED.

XXI. The certificate upon which permits are granted, attached to copies of the invoices permitted, shall be filed by the officer granting the permit.

EXCEPTED ARTICLES.

XXII. Fresh vegetables, fruits, butter and eggs, ice, poultry, coal, wood, beef cattle, hogs, and household goods of families moving, may be permitted by the officers named in Regulation II to go to any military post, naval fleet or vessel of the United States forces, other than within or attached to the blockade, without the supply store authority and certificate above required. But in such cases the permit shall be conditioned that the supplies so permitted shall be reported to the Assistant or Local Special Agent at such post, fleet, or vessel, if there be such an officer there, and if not, then to the commanding officer of the post, fleet, or vessel, and that the same shall be disposed of only in compliance with these Regulations.

SUTLERS' PERMITS.

XXIII. Permits will be granted to Sutlers to transport to the regiments or post sutlered by them such articles as they are authorized to sell, free of the three per cent. fee; but no permit will be granted to a Sutler except on presentation, to the proper permit officer, of the original certificate of his appointment from the commanding officer of his regiment or post, countersigned by the Division commander thereof, and an application and affidavit in the following form:

AFFIDAVIT OF SUTLER.

...., being duly sworn, deposes and says, that .... is the Sutler of the ...., duly appointed and commissioned in writing, a true copy of which appointment is hereto annexed; that there is no other person claiming to act as Sutler to said ...., to the knowledge of this affiant; that no other goods, wares, or merchandize, have been transported to said ...., under this commission, except such as have been duly permitted, and that a memorandum of each shipment permitted is endorsed on said commission, and truly appears on the copy thereof hereto attached; that no goods, wares, or merchandise transported under such permits have been sold to any persons except the officers or soldiers belonging to said .... or other forces of the United States, and that none of those permitted under this application shall be so sold.

Subscribed and sworn to before me }
this .... day of ...., 186... }

AMOUNT PERMITTED TO SUTLERS.

XXIV. Transportation under the above Regulation shall not be permitted to any regimental Sutler for an amount of goods exceeding $2,500 per month; nor for over two months supply at one time; nor for any goods except such as he is by law and War Department orders allowed to deal in; nor to any post Sutler to an amount larger than shall be stated in his commission and approved by the General commanding the Department or Division, and in such cases only one months' supply shall be permitted at one time.

RESTRICTIONS ON CARRIERS.

XXV. No vessel, boat, or other vehicle, used for transportation from any place in the loyal States, shall carry goods, wares, or merchandise into any place, section, or State not declared in insurrection, but with which commercial intercourse has been or may be restricted, without the permit of a duly authorized officer of the Treasury Department, application for which permit may be made to such authorized officer near the point of destination, as may suit the convenience of the shipper. Nor shall any vessel, boat, or other craft, or vehicle used for transportation, put off any goods, wares, or merchancise, at any place other than that named in the permit or clearance as the place of destination of such goods, wares and merchandise.

BOATS ON WESTERN WATERS.

XXVI. Before any boat or vessel running on any of the western waters south of Cairo, or other waters within or adjacent to any State or section, commercial intercourse with which now is, or may hereafter be, restricted, as aforesaid, shall depart from any port where there is a collector or surveyor of customs, there shall be exhibited to the collector or surveyor, or such other officer as may be authorized to act in his stead, a true manifest of its entire cargo, and a clearance, obtained to proceed on its voyage; and when freights are received on board at a place where there is no Collector or Surveyor, as hereinafter provided in Regulation XXVII, then the same exhibit shall be made and clearance obtained at the first port to be passed where there is such an officer, if required by him, and such vessel or boat shall be reported and the manifest of its cargo exhibited to the collector or surveyor of every port to be passed on the trip where there is such an officer, if required by him; but no new clearance shall be necessary unless additional freights shall have been taken on board after the last clearance. Immediately on arriving at the port of final destination, and before discharging any part of the cargo, the manifest shall be exhibited to the Surveyor of such port, or other officer authorized to act in his stead, whose approval for landing the cargo shall be indorsed on the manifest before any part thereof shall be discharged; and the clearance and shipping permits of all such vessels and boats shall be exhibited to the officer in command of any naval vessel or military post, whenever such officer may require it.

AGENCY AIDS.

XXVII. To facilitate trade, and guard against improper transportation, Agency Aids will be appointed by the proper Supervising Special Agent, or, under his direction, by an Assistant Special Agent, from time to time, on cars, vessels, and boats, when desired by owners, agents, or masters thereof, which Aids will have free carriage on the respective cars, vessels, and boats on which they are placed, and will allow proper way freights to be taken on board without permit, keeping a statement thereof, and reporting the same to the first officer to be passed on the trip who is authorized to grant the permit desired, from whom a permit therefor must be obtained, or the goods shall be returned to the shipper under his direction. No permit will be granted for transportation into or within any State or district under restriction, or declared in insurrection, except on cars, vessels, and boats carrying such Aids, or by private conveyance specified in the permit, or on boats, vessels, or cars bonded not to receive anything on board for transportation during the trip, nor to land or discharge anything at any point, except that of ultimate destination, without proper permit.

MERCHANDISE LIABLE TO REACH INSURGENTS—BOND REQUIRED.

XXVIII. When any Collector, Surveyor, Supervising, Assistant, or Local Special Agent, charged with the execution of these Regulations, and the laws authorizing them, shall find within his proper limits any goods, wares, or merchandise which, in his opinion, founded on satisfactory evidence in writing, are in danger of being transported to insurgents, he may require the owner or holder thereof to give reasonable security that they shall not be transported to any place under insurrectionary control, and shall not, in any way, be used to give aid or encouragement to the insurgents.

If the required security be not given, such officer shall promptly state the facts to the United States Marshal for the district within which such goods are situated; or, if there be no United States Marshal, then to the commander of a near military post, whose duty it shall be to take possession thereof, and hold them for safe-keeping, reporting the facts promptly to the Secretary of the Treasury, and awaiting instructions.

ARTICLES PROHIBITED BY MILITARY ORDER.

XXIX. When any military order, issued by competent authority, shall absolutely prohibit the transportation of articles designated therein, to, or within any State or part of State named in the order, no permit shall be granted for the transportation so prohibited. But when such prohibition is conditional, transportation may be permitted in accordance with the conditions named.

PACKAGES TO OFFICERS AND SOLDIERS.

XXX. In cases where military or naval Commanders shall have ordered all packages sent by friends to the officers and soldiers of their command, to be delivered only to designated regimental or vessel officers for delivery to the proper parties, such packages may be transported, without Collector's or Surveyor's permits, by the Adams Express Company, or other carriers having authority for that purpose from the Secretary of the Treasury, on such carriers giving bond conditioned to render a true account of all such packages by them transported, and to carry no goods without proper permits, other than such packages.

ARMY AND NAVY SUPPLIES.

XXXI. Supplies and other property belonging to the United States for the use of the army or navy, moving under military or naval orders, are excepted from the operation of these Regulations. Supplies for the army or navy, furnished under contract, will be permitted free of charge, upon the certificate of the proper military or naval officer that such supplies are required, and are to be shipped in fulfilment of an actual existing contract with the Government.

COIN OR BULLION.

XXXII. All transportation of coin or bullion to any State or section heretofore declared to be in insurrection is absolutely prohibited, except for military purposes, and under military orders, or under the special license of the President.

BLOCKADED PORTS.

XXXIII. Clearances and permits to any port or place affected by the existing blockade will be granted only upon the request of the Department of War or the Department of the Navy. Applicants must present, with their application, a certificate from the Department of War, or Department of the Navy, either directly or through a duly authorized officer, that the articles are required for military or naval purposes, and a request that the transportation of the same may be permitted, together with invoices in duplicate of the articles to be permitted, specifying their character, quantity, value, and destination. On receiving such certificate and request and duplicate invoices, the Secretary of the Treasury, or some officer specially authorized by him, will transmit to the proper officer one of the invoices, and direct the permitting of the transportation requested, and forward the other invoice to the Assistant or Local Special Agent at the port or place to which the goods are to be permitted, who will, in all cases, on the arrival of any articles claimed to have been permitted, examine and compare such articles with the duplicate invoices; and in case of any excess or evasion of the permit, he will seize the whole shipment, and report the facts forthwith to the Supervising Special Agent, that proceedings may be taken for their forfeiture under the acts of July 13, 1861, May 20, 1862, March 12, 1863, and July 2, 1864.

BLOCKADED PORTS REOPENED.

XXXIV. Where ports heretofore blockaded have been opened by proclamation of the President, licenses will be granted by United States Consuls, on application by the proper parties, to vessels clearing from foreign ports to the ports so opened, upon satisfactory evidence that the vessel so licensed will convey no person, property, or information contraband of war, either to or from said ports, which license shall be shown to the Collector of the port to which the vessel is bound, and, if required, to any officer in charge of the block-ade. And on leaving any port so opened, the vessel must have a clearance from the Collector, according to law, showing no violation of the conditions of the license. Any violation of the conditions will involve the forfeiture and condemnation of the vessel and cargo, and the exclusion of all parties concerned from entering the United States for any purpose during the war.

Vessels clearing from domestic ports to any of the ports so opened, will apply to the custom-house officers of the proper ports, in the usual manner, for permits and clearances under the Regulations heretofore established.

Commercial intercourse between the citizens of ports so opened and persons beyond the limits thereof, shall be subject the same restrictions and regulations, as at other places in States and parts of States declared in insurrection.

REFUSAL OF CLEARANCE.

XXXV. Collectors and Surveyors will refuse clearances and per-mits to all vessels or other vehicles laden with goods, wares, or merchandise destined for a foreign or domestic port, whenever they shall have satisfactory reason to believe that such goods, wares, or merchandise, or any part thereof, whatever may be their ostensible destination, are intended for ports or places in possession or under control of insurgents against the United States. And if any vessel or other vehicle for which a clearance or permit shall have been refused, as aforesaid, shall depart, or attempt to depart, for a foreign or domestic port, without being duly cleared or permitted, such Col-lector or Surveyor, or the Supervising Special Agent, or Assistant Special Agent, shall cause such vessel or vehicle to be seized and detained, and proceedings to be instituted for the forfeiture to the United States of such vessel or other vehicle, with her tackle, apparel, furniture, and cargo.

BONDS FOR CLEARANCE.

XXXVI. Whenever application is made to a Collector, or Sur-veyor authorized to grant it, for a permit or clearance, for either a foreign or domestic port, if, for satisfactory reasons, he shall deem it necessary to prevent the cargo of the vessel from being used in affording aid and comfort to any person or parties in insurrection against the authority of the United States, he shall require a bond to be executed by the master or owner of the vessel, in a penalty equal to the value of the cargo, and with sureties to the satisfaction of such Collector or Surveyor, conditioned that the said cargo shall be deliv-ered at the destination for which it is cleared or permitted, and that no part thereof shall be used in affording aid or comfort to any person or parties in insurrection against the authority of the United States, with the knowledge or consent or connivance of the owner or shipper thereof, or with the knowledge, consent, or connivance of the master of the vessel on which the same may be laden, or of other persons having control of the same.

VESSELS TO REPORT.

XXXVII. Every vessel, on approaching a gunboat or revenue cutter, or vessel appearing to be such, before proceeding further, shall bear up and speak said boat or cutter, and submit to such examination as may be required.

TRANSPORTATION OF PRODUCTS.

XXXVIII. All loyal persons residing in a State or part of a State declared in insurrection, if, within the lines of actual occupation by the military forces of the United States, as indicated by the published order of the Commanding General of the Department or District so occupied, may be permitted by the Supervising Special Agent thereof, or such Assistant Special Agent as he shall designate for that purpose, to bring or send to market in the loyal States any products which they shall have produced with their own labor, or the labor of freedmen or others employed and paid by them, upon making and filing with such officer an affidavit in the following form :

AFFIDAVIT OF APPLICANT TO TRANSPORT PRODUCTS.

State of.............. .... }
   County of........................... } *ss :*

   I, ..., being duly sworn, say, that I reside in the county of....... .... in the State of........ .. ..; that I have produced during the year 186 , ... with my own labor and the labor of freedmen and others whom I have employed and paid or secured to be paid, according to the rules of the Supervising Special Agent of the .... Agency ; that I desire to transport the same to...........................in the State of........ ...., by way of......... ...., for sale, or other disposition : that the same is now at............ ...., in the county of.................... ......, and State of ...., and is contained in............ packages, marked......... ....; that I am in all respects true and loyal to the Government of the United States, and have never committed any act by which my property is rendered liable to forfeiture or confiscation to the United States, under any law thereof.

   Subscribed and sworn to before me }
       this...................... ....186 . }

PERMIT TO TRANSPORT PRODUCTS.

XXXIX. Upon receiving the above affidavit and being satisfied of its truth, such Agent shall grant a permit authorizing the transportation of the products named, to the first port or place, in a loyal State where there is a permit officer named in Regulation II, and at which the same are to be unladed or reshipped, which place shall be named in the permit.   Such permit shall be in the following form :

.... having made application to me for permit to transport .... from ...., in the County of ....,
and State of...... ...., to ...., in the State of ...., by way of

...., and having made and filed with me the affidavit prescribed for such cases, and given bond with approved sureties for the payment of all fees and Government dues upon the said ...., upon its arrival at .... aforesaid, permission is hereby given to the said .... to transport the said .... which is contained in .... packages marked ...., from .... aforesaid to .... aforesaid.

Dated at ...., this .... day of ...., 186...

BOND TO TRANSPORT PRODUCTS.

XL. Before delivering the permit, the Agent granting it shall require and receive from the applicant his bond to the United States in duplicate, with two or more sureties, to be approved by him, in a penalty of twice the value of the products so permitted to be transported, in the following form:

Know all men by these presents, That we ....,
of .... as principal, and ....,
of .... , and ...., of ....,
as sureties, are held and firmly bound unto the United States of America in the sum of
....dollars, ($...............,) to be paid to the United States of America;
for which payment, well and truly to be made, we bind ourselves, our heirs, executors, and administrators, jointly and severally, firmly by these presents. Sealed with our seals, and dated this .... day of ...., in the year one thousand, eight hundred and sixty-.................
Whereas the said .... has applied for and received a permit to transport
.... from ...., in the County of ....,
n the State of ...., to .... , in the State of ...., by way of ...., which .... is contained in .... packages
marked ....,

Now the condition of the above obligation is such, That if the said
.... shall transport the said .. .. to ....
aforesaid, and there report it to the .... of Customs and pay all fees and Government dues upon the same, and if, in all things connected therewith, he shall comply with the laws and with the Regulations of the Secretary of the Treasury concerning the same, then this obligation to be void; otherwise to remain in full force and virtue.

In presence of—

—— ——, [L. S.]
—— ——, [L. S.]
—— ——, [L. S.]

DISPOSITION OF BOND.

XLI. Upon receiving the duplicate bond above required, the Agent shall forthwith send the original to the officer of the port to whom the fees are to be paid, and inform him of any facts relating to the shipment and transportation which may enable him more certainly to secure the collection of Government fees and dues, and upon arrival of the products at his port, such officer shall collect the prescribed fees, and inform the Internal Revenue officer, that he may collect the tax upon it. When these payments are made, he shall cancel the bond, by writing across its face "cancelled," and shall sign his name thereto, and deliver it to the maker or his representative. The Agent who received the bond shall, upon presentation to him of the bond so cancelled, also cancel the duplicate in his possession in the same manner, but shall retain the same so cancelled.

TRANSHIPMENT OF PRODUCTS.

XLII. If, from any cause, it becomes necessary to tranship any products *in transitu* under permit, as above provided, notice thereof shall be given to the permit officer of the port or place where it is made, or, if made where there is no such officer, then at the first port or place to be passed where there is one, and obtain his approval of the transhipment, to be indorsed on the permit. The officer so approving will promptly advise the proper officer at the port of destination of his action in the premises.

PLANTATION SUPPLIES.

XLIII. Stock, implements and supplies, for plantations worked by freedmen under the Regulations relating thereto, may be permitted to be transported to such plantations without payment of the fees hereafter prescribed, upon presentation to the permit officer of a certificate of the Supervising Special Agent, or Assistant Special Agent of the district in which they are located, in the following form :

CERTIFICATE FOR PLANTATION SUPPLIES.

This may certify that .... is a loyal person residing in the county of .... in the State of .... within the lines of actual occupation by the military forces of the United States, and that he is working the plantation known as the .... in the .... of .... and State of ...., and that he employs .... freedmen thereon, under the Regulations of the Secretary of the Treasury relating thereto: that the articles and supplies named in the memorandum thereof, countersigned by me, and hereto attached, are necessary in carrying on the said plantation and supporting the freedmen and their families thereon.

Dated at .... this......... day of 186

—— ——, *Special Agent,*

...........................*Agency.*

PRODUCTS MOVING WITHOUT PERMIT TO BE SEIZED.

XLIV. Officers and Agents of the Treasury Department are directed to seize any products of an insurrectionary State, found moving without permit as above provided, or without evidence that all fees and Government dues have been paid, and to cause proceedings to be instituted for the forfeiture thereof to the United States.

FORFEITURE FOR VIOLATIONS.

XLV. All vessels, boats, and other vehicles used for transportation, violating Regulations or local rules, and all cotton, tobacco, or other products or merchandise shipped or transported, or purchased or sold in violation thereof, will be forfeited to the United

States. If any false statement be made or deception practiced in obtaining an authority, certificate, or permit under these Regulations, such authority, certificate, or permit, and all others connected therewith or affected thereby, will be absolutely void, and all merchandise purchased or shipped under them shall be forfeited to the United States. In all cases of forfeiture, as aforesaid, immediate seizure will be made and proceedings instituted promptly for condemnation. The attention of all officers of the Government, common-carriers, shippers, consignees, owners, masters, conductors, agents, drivers, and other persons connected with the transportation of merchandise, or trading therein, is particularly directed to the acts of July 13, 1861, May 20, 1862, March 12. 1863, and July 2, 1864, and to the orders of the Secretaries of War and of the Navy hereto appended.

FEES.

XLVI. The following fees are prescribed:

Fees for administering oath and certifying affidavit............... 10 cents.
" Authority from Agent............... 3 dolls.
" Certificate of Assistant or Local Special Agent............... 10 cents.
" Each permit for purposes of trade............... 20 "
" Each permit to transport cotton from any insurrectionary district to any loyal State, per pound, ... 4 cents.
" Permit to transport tobacco, per hhd,............... 2 dolls.
" Permit to transport to or from such district, other products, goods, wares, or merchandise, three per centum on the sworn invoice value thereof at the place of shipment.
" For each permit for individual, family or plantation supplies, on every purchase over $20 and not over $50............... 5 cents.
" Over $50 and not over $100............... 10 "
" Over $100............... 15 "

For permits for individual, family, or plantation supplies, not over twenty dollars in amount, no charge is allowed, except for revenue stamps, on affida its and certificates in districts under restriction; and no charge, except five cents for permit and five cents for each revenue stamp on affidavit and certificate, is allowed in States declared in insurrection. When purchases are less than five dollars, the permit officer may dispense with affidavits and certificates, when no ground to suspect fraud or imposition appears.

Internal revenue stamps are required by law to be attached to affidavits, certificates, and bonds, but not to any other instruments or writings provided for by these Regulations. Stamps will be furnished by the proper Special Agents at the rates fixed by the internal revenue act, namely:

Affidavit............... 5
Bonds not exceeding $1000............... 50
" exceeding $1000, for every additional $1000 or fractional part thereof............... 50
Certificates............... 5
Power of Attorney............... 50

XLVII. Every officer authorized by the Secretary of the Treasury to grant permits under Regulation II, shall keep in his office a record of every permit granted by him, showing the names of the owner, shipper, and consignee, the place from and to which each transportation is permitted, the character and invoice value of the merchandise permitted, and shall transmit to the Secretary as nearly as possible on the first day of every month, an abstract of such record and an abstract statement, showing the permits granted daily to parts of States not declared in insurrection, but in which trade is restricted, and also showing the number and aggregate amount of permits granted daily to States declared in insurrection, the fees received, and the disposition made of the same, together with the names of all Agency Aids reporting to him, and the compensation paid to each.

AGENTS TO PAY OVER MONEY, &c.

XLVIII. All money received by each Assistant or Local Special Agent shall be paid over as promptly as possible to the Supervising Special Agent, or to an Assistant Treasurer, or Designated Depository, as directed by him, and so that all receipts during each month shall be paid over before the making of his required monthly report; and all money received by each Supervising Special Agent, or Collector, Surveyor, or other officer authorized to grant permits, under these Regulations, shall be promptly paid over to the Assistant Treasurer, or Designated Depository most convenient to him, and so that all receipts for each month shall be so paid over, before the making of his monthly report.

OFFICERS TO REPORT.

XLIX. Every officer authorized to receive money under these Regulations shall transmit to the Secretary, on the first of each month, a report, stating in detail all moneys so received by him during the preceding month, and from what sources received, together with all expenses of his office incidental to the execution of these Regulations; and if any money has been paid out or otherwise disposed of by him during the month, an account thereof, and by what authority, to whom, or for what purpose it was so paid or disposed of, with the vouchers therefor. A duplicate of this report and account, when made by officers in States declared in insurrection, or in restricted districts in loyal States, shall, at the same time, be transmitted to the Supervising Special Agent for the Agency in which it shall be made.

RECORDS—LOCAL SPECIAL AGENTS.

L. Local Special Agents shall keep a record of every permit and certificate given by them, with the date and amount thereof, and the name and residence of the party to whom given; of all bonds required of owners or holders of goods in danger of being transported to insurgents, and their action where the required bond is not given. And they will also, as nearly as possible on the first day of every month, transmit to the proper Supervising Special Agent a transcript of such record, and will deliver to such Agent all bonds or securities received by them under these Regulations.

RECORDS—ASSISTANT SPECIAL AGENTS.

LI. Assistant Special Agents shall keep a record of all their official transactions, showing specifically and in detail every authority given to sell supplies; every authority for the transportation of products; every inspection of a supply store, and the results thereof; all appointments of Agency Aids on cars, vessels, and boats, and the compensation of each; all seizures in cases of excess or evasion of permits to blockaded ports; all seizures or detentions of vessels or vehicles departing, or attempting to depart, when clearance has been refused; all cases of security required when goods found in danger of being transported to insurgents, and if security not given, the action taken by them; all fees received for affidavits and authorities to sell supplies, and for the transportation of products, and from whom and for what received. And they shall, on the first day of every month, transmit to the proper Supervising Special Agent a transcript of such record, and all bonds or securities received by them under these Regulations.

RECORDS—SUPERVISING SPECIAL AGENTS.

LII. Supervising Special Agents shall keep a record of all their official transactions, showing fully the name and location of each Local Special Agent and Agency Aid appointed by them, and the compensation of each; of conferences with Generals commanding Departments, and designations of military lines, (Reg. IV;) of all authorities given for supply stores, stating the date, name of trader, and amount of goods authorized; of the inspection of supply stores and the results; of all authorities given for the transportation of products, to whom given, and the locality from which and to which transportation is permitted; of all revocations of authorities, certificates, and permits; of all information touching any goods or transactions given to other officers of the department; of all appointments of Agency Aids upon cars, vessels, and boats; of all seizures and detentions of vessels or vehicles departing or attempting to depart, after clearance has been refused; of all securities required and received of owners or holders of goods in danger of being transported to insurgents, and of their action if security was not given. And on the first day of every month, as nearly as possible, they shall transmit to this Department an abstract of such record for the previous month, together with a copy of the abstracts of records, and a statement of all bonds and securities received by them from Assistant and Local Special Agents.

GENERAL AGENT.

LIII. The General Agent will visit the several Agencies and permit officers, as often as practicable, and take or direct such action as may be necessary to insure a uniform construction of these Regulations, and harmony of action under them; direct the making of such local Rules by Supervising Special Agents, as in his judgment shall be proper; hear and decide, or refer to the Secretary of the Treasury, appeals from the action of the Supervising or other Special Agents; and generally to cause the laws and regulations governing restricted intercourse to be faithfully and honestly administered. And he shall promptly report to the Secretary of the Treasury all misconduct or inefficiency on the part of Supervising, Assistant, or other Agents and officers engaged in executing these Regulations.

THESE REGULATIONS TO SUPERSEDE ALL OTHERS.

LIV. These Regulations shall supersede those of September 11, 1863, and all others conflicting herewith, affecting commercial intercourse with States declared in insurrection; and all permits hereafter granted by any officer of the Treasury Department will be granted in pursuance of them, and of the Local Rules authorized by them, or by virtue of authority hereafter given by the Secretary of the Treasury.

AUTHORITIES REVOKED.

LV. All existing authorities to purchase products in insurrectionary States are hereby revoked, except that products purchased in good faith under such authorities, and paid for prior to the date hereof, may be transported, in the same manner and subject to the same conditions as products raised by the labor of freedmen. (Reg. XXXVIII.)

All authorities to transport goods, wares, or merchandise into an insurrectionary State are hereby revoked.

WHEN REGULATIONS TAKE EFFECT.

LVI. These Regulations shall take effect upon the publication thereof.

ABANDONED, CAPTURED, AND CONFISCABLE PERSONAL PROPERTY.

REGULATIONS.

PRESCRIBED BY THE SECRETARY OF THE TREASURY CONCERNING ABAN-
DONED, CAPTURED, AND CONFISCABLE PROPERTY, UNDER THE ACTS OF
CONGRESS RESPECTIVELY APPROVED MARCH 12, 1863, AND JULY 2, 1864.

AGENTS TO CARRY OUT THESE REGULATIONS.

I. The Regulations relative to abandoned, captured, and confiscable personal property will be carried into effect by the same Agents, and under the same supervision, as are provided under the Regulations concerning commercial intercourse.

ASSISTANT SPECIAL AGENTS IN EACH AGENCY.

II. There shall be assigned to each Special Agency such number of Assistant Special Agents as may be necessary, who, with the Supervising Special Agent, shall collect and receive all abandoned, captured, and confiscable property, except such as has been used or was intended to be used for waging or carrying on war against the United States, viz: arms, ordnance, ships, steamboats, or other watercraft, and their furniture, forage, military supplies, and munitions of war.

ABANDONED, CAPTURED, AND CONFISCABLE PROPERTY DESCRIBED.

III. Abandoned property is that which has been or may be deserted by the owners, or when the lawful owner thereof shall be voluntarily absent therefrom and engaged, either in arms or otherwise, in aiding or encouraging the rebellion.

Captured property is that which has been or may be seized or taken from hostile possession by the military or naval forces of the United States.

Confiscable property is that which is liable to confiscation under the act of July 17, 1862.

AGENTS TO KEEP RECORDS.

IV. Each agent collecting or receiving any such property, will immediately make and keep a full record of all the facts or information concerning it, known or accessible to him, including, as nearly as possible, the following: the character and quantity of the property received or collected; where captured, or found, or received as abandoned; under what circumstances; by whom owned or alleged to be owned; noting, where practicable, the name and address of one or more truthful residents in the neighborhood acquainted with the property and the owner or claimant thereof, and any statements they may make in connection therewith; by whom such property was captured, abandoned, or seized for confiscation; by whom received or collected; from whom received; all names, marks, signs, or devices, (whether distinct, indistinct, or partially erased,) upon such property; together with all other information which may in any way serve to identify or make known the history of any particular lot, or to trace the same, or the proceeds thereof, from the earliest period possible to its final disposition.

He will also charge against each lot and keep a true and detailed account in triplicate of each item of expense incurred in its collection, transportation, care and sale or other disposition by him, or where two or more lots are treated together, a fair and just proportion against each, as well as all fees due, in any way, to the Government thereon.

AGENTS TO MAKE REPORTS.

V. When such property is collected or received by an Assistant Special Agent, he will promptly transmit one copy of the above record to the Secretary of the Treasury, and one to the proper Supervising Special Agent, and will retain one copy for his own files. When it is so collected or received by a Supervising Special Agent, he will transmit one copy of the record to the Secretary of the Treasury and retain one copy for his own files.

AGENTS TO RECEIVE AND COLLECT ABANDONED PERSONAL PROPERTY AND GIVE RECEIPTS.

VI. Such Agents will receive and collect abandoned personal property from any officer or private of the regular or volunteer forces of the United States, or any officer, sailor, or marine in the naval service of the United States, upon the inland waters of the United States, who may have, take, or receive any abandoned property from persons in such insurrectionary districts, or have it under their control, and the Agent receiving it will in all cases give a receipt therefor in the following form:

Received .... of ....,
.... estimated
at $..................... ...., taken or received and held by him as abandoned property in an insurrectionary district, and claimed to be the property of ....
..................................., and turned over to me by said ....,
which property I have received as Agent of the Treasury Department, appointed in pursuance of certain acts of Congress, approved July 13, 1861, May 20, 1862, March 12, 1863, and July 2, 1864.

The said property to be transported and disposed of under the Regulations of the Secretary of the Treasury prescribed in pursuance of the authority conferred on him by said acts.

Dated ...., 186...

And a record of the property so collected and received shall be made, and the property disposed of as directed in Regulations IV, IX, XI, and XV.

AGENTS TO RECEIVE PROPERTY FROM PERSONS IN MILITARY OR NAVAL SERVICE.

VII. Such Agents will collect and receive of any officer or private, or person employed in, or with the regular or volunteer forces of the United States, any property held by him which shall have been captured in any district declared to be in insurrection against the United States, except such as shall be required for military use of the United States forces; and all property so held by them shall be received by the Agent as captured property, leaving all questions concerning the class to which it belongs for the consideration of the Secretary of the Treasury; and they shall also receive with such property the necessary invoices thereof, and all receipts, bills of lading, and other papers, documents, and vouchers, showing title to such property or the right to the possession, control, or direction thereof, and such order, indorsement, or writing as the party has power to make, to enable such Agent to take possession of such property or the proceeds thereof.

And he will give to the officer, private, or person from whom any property is so received, a receipt in the form following:

"Received of ....,
estimated at $.. captured by the forces of the United States, and claimed to be the property of .... which property I have received as Special Agent of the Treasury Department, appointed in pursuance of certain acts of Congress, approved July 13, 1861, May 20, 1862, March 12, 1863, and July 2, 1864. The said property to be transported and disposed of under the regulations of the Secretary of the Treasury prescribed in pursuance of the authority conferred on him by said acts."

And a record of the property so collected and received shall be made, and copies transmitted, and the property disposed of, as directed in Regulations IV, IX, XI, and XV.

PROPERTY REQUIRED FOR PUBLIC USE TO BE APPRAISED AND DELIVERED OVER.

VIII. When any part of the goods or property received or collected by any Supervising or Assistant Special Agent is demanded for public use, and a requisition therefor is presented, signed by the General commanding Department, or by some other officer authorized by such Commander of Department, the Special Agent having such property in charge shall select three competent and disinterested persons, to be approved by such officer, who shall make oath for the faithful discharge of their duties, and who shall appraise said

3

goods or property, and make a certificate thereof in the following form :

The undersigned having been appointed by .... Special Agent, to appraise certain property alleged to have been collected or received as abandoned or captured by .... Special Agent of the Treasury Department, having each of us made oath for the faithful discharge of our duty as such appraisers, do certify that we have carefully examined and appraised the following described property, to wit :.................................... .... and that said property is worth ....

$$\left.\begin{array}{l} \underline{\qquad} \quad \underline{\qquad} \\ \underline{\qquad} \quad \underline{\qquad} \\ \underline{\qquad} \quad \underline{\qquad} \end{array}\right\} \ \textit{Appraisers.}$$

Which certificate shall be certified by the Special Agent and by the officer receiving said property ; and the goods or property so appraised shall be delivered over to the officer appointed to receive it ; and the Special Agent shall in all such cases require from the officer or agent receiving said goods or property a receipt in the following form :

Received of .... alleged to have been collected or received by him as abandoned or captured, and which has been this day appraised by .... appraisers appointed with my approval, to be worth .... dollars, which property has been delivered to me by said agent to be appropriated to the public use, as provided in the second section of the Act of Congress, approved March 12, 1863, entitled " An act to provide for the collection of abandoned property, and the prevention of frauds in insurrectionary districts within the United States. "

And he shall keep a record of all expenses incurred on account thereof, with a full description of all such property, and shall make a full report of such appraisal proceedings to the Secretary of the Treasury, and transmit therewith copies of all papers in the case, and if an Assistant Special Agent, he shall send copies of the report and all other papers in the case to the proper Supervising Special Agent.

DISPOSITION OF PERISHABLE PROPERTY AND SUCH AS CANNOT BE TRANSPORTED.

IX. In all cases where captured and abandoned property of a perishable nature shall be collected or received by the proper Agents of this Department, and its immediate sale is required by the interest of all concerned, such Agent shall, where practicable, forward it without delay to the nearest place designated by the Secretary or by Regulation as a place of sale within a loyal State, consigned to the proper officer of this Department, who shall forthwith cause it to be sold at auction to the highest bidder ; all such shipments to be accompanied by a statement as required by Regulation IV.

If, from the character of the property, it shall be impracticable so to transport it, the Agent shall cause the same to be appraised by three disinterested persons, and to be sold at public auction, and promptly transmit a full report, as prescribed by Regulation IV. together with the certificate of appraisal, taken in triplicate, and the account of sales, and hold the proceeds subject to the direction of the Supervising Special Agent for that Agency.

CONTRACTS FOR COLLECTION AND DELIVERY OF PROPERTY.

X. When property is liable to be lost or destroyed, in consequence of its location being unknown to the Special Agents, or from other causes, and parties propose, for compensation, to collect and deliver it into the hands of such agents, at points designated by them, Supervising Special Agents may contract, on behalf of the United States, for the collection and delivery to them of such property in their respective agencies, on the best possible terms, not exceeding twenty-five per cent. of the proceeds of the property, which percentage must be full compensation for all expenses, of whatever character, incurred in collecting, preparing, and delivering such property at the points designated. Prior to any such contract being made, the party proposing must submit in writing a statement of the kind and amount of property proposed to be collected, the locality whence to be obtained, and all the facts and circumstances connected with it, particularly as to its ownership. And any contract made in pursuance of this Regulation must be in writing, and restricted to the collection and delivery of particular lots at named localities ; or, when circumstances clearly justify it, to the general collection and delivery of all abandoned property in limited districts not greater in any case than one parish or county, and not more than one district to be assigned to one contractor.

Before payment to any contractor under any contract made in pursuance of this regulation, he shall execute a bond, with penalty equal to the amount stipulated to be paid to him, and with sureties satisfactory to the Supervising Special Agent, indemnifying the United States against all claims to the property delivered on account of damages by trespass, or otherwise occasioned by the act or connivance of the contractor, and against all claims that may arise on account of expenses incurred in the collection, preparation, and transportation of said property to the points designated in said contract.

Should a case arise in the opinion of the Supervising Special Agent justifying the payment of a larger percentage than one quarter of the proceeds of the property, he will make a statement of the facts and circumstances and the reasons in his opinion justifying such additional allowance, and refer the same to the Secretary for instructions.

And for the purpose of getting possession of and transporting to market as much of the captured and abandoned property as possible, Supervising Special Agents, or Assistant Special Agents under their direction, will appoint and employ in their respective Agencies, at such per diem compensation as may be judged proper, subject to approval of the Secretary of the Treasury, such Local Special Agents and

Agency Aids as may be necessary therefor, instructing them fully as to the execution of the duties respectively assigned to them.

DISPOSITION OF CONFISCABLE PROPERTY.

XI. All confiscable personal property collected or received in any Agency shall forthwith be forwarded to the Supervising Special Agent thereof, or as directed by him to the proper officer of the Treasury Department, at the port or place to which it shall be sent for legal proceedings, under the Act of July 17, 1862; and upon presentation to such officer by the United States Marshal of the proper writ in such proceedings, issued by a court of competent jurisdiction, the said property shall be delivered to him. Upon making such delivery, the officer delivering will require from the Marshal duplicate receipts therefor in the following form:

Received of ...., Supervising Special Agent, appointed to collect and receive confiscable property, as provided in the Act of Congress, approved July 2, 1864, the following described property, viz : ....
which it is alleged belonged to...... ...., of ...., in the State of...... ....,
whose property, it is charged, is confiscable under the Act of Congress approved July 17, 1862.

By virtue of a writ issued by the .... Court, in proceedings therein for the condemnation of said property, under the last-named act, I have demanded and received the same.

Dated .... 186 .

RECORD TO BE KEPT OF CONFISCABLE PROPERTY.

XII. Agents collecting and receiving such property will be careful to ascertain and record, in addition to the requirements of Regulation IV, all allegations against the owner of the property, together with the names and residences of witnesses by whom they can be sustained, and all other facts relating thereto which may tend to secure justice under the law ; and will transmit one copy thereof to the United States District Attorney, who is to institute proceedings for confiscation.

CAPTURED, ABANDONED, OR CONFISCABLE PROPERTY TO BE RE-LEASED ONLY BY AUTHORITY OF SECRETARY.

XIII. No property collected or received as captured, abandoned, or confiscable under any act of Congress shall be released by any Agent, except by special authority from the Secretary of the Treasury, to any persons claiming ownership of such property; nor shall any permit be given by such Agents to individuals to remove such property; nor shall any liability be incurred or assumed, or contract be made on the part of the United States by such Agents, except as authorized by these Regulations. No personal favor shall in any case be extended to one individual or party rather than another.

ASSISTANT AGENTS TO FORWARD PROPERTY.

XIV. All abandoned, captured, or confiscable property, collected or received by an Assistant Special Agent, will be promptly forwarded by him to the Supervising Special Agent of the Agency in which it shall be collected or received, or to such place of sale as he may direct. And all such property collected or received by a Supervising Special Agent shall be by him either sold or forwarded for sale in compliance with instructions to him from the Secretary of the Treasury or from the General Agent of the Treasury Department.

DISPOSITION OF PERSONAL PROPERTY.

XV. All personal property collected and received, in compliance with these Regulations, other than such as may be appropriated to public use, shall be transported to such places as shall be designated by the Secretary of the Treasury, as places of sale, consigned to the Supervising Special Agent of the Agency in which it is collected or received, if within his Agency, or to such other person, as shall be specially authorized by the Secretary to receive the same, and shall there be sold by such Supervising Special Agent, or other person, at public auction to the highest bidder, for lawful money, pursuant to notice previously published of the time and place of sale.

PAYMENT OF EXPENSES OF PROPERTY.

XVI. Supervising Special Agents, and such other persons as shall be specially authorized by the Secretary of the Treasury to receive and sell captured, abandoned, and confiscable property, will pay or cause to be paid, out of the general fund arising from the sale of all such property received and sold by him, all expenses necessarily incurred in collecting, receiving, securing, and disposing of the same, including fees, taxes, freights, storage, charges, labor, and other necessary expenses, being careful to avoid all useless or indiscreet expenditures; and will charge each particular lot or parcel with the specific or proportionate amount of all such expenses as can be made specific or proportionate charges to each lot or parcel; and will also charge and retain out of the proceeds of each lot or parcel one and one half per centum thereof for the payment of such expenses connected with the collection, transportation, and sale, or other disposition thereof, as cannot be made specific or proportionate charges against each lot or parcel, or are not otherwise provided for, such as rents, compensation to clerks, or other employés, auctioneers, printing, and advertising, a carefully stated account of which will be kept by such Agents, or other persons, showing in detail all expenses paid out of this fund arising from such charge; and unless unavoidably prevented, they will take vouchers for all expenditures made under this Regulation, and transmit the same with their accounts to the Secretary of the Treasury. Out of the balance, if any, of said one and one half per centum remaining after defraying said expenses the several Supervising Special Agents, or other persons selling as afore-said, may retain as compensation for extra care and responsibility a sum not exceeding three fourths of one per centum of the amount of such sales; and with the remainder, if any, may reward extra ser-vices in the collection and care of property, rendered by Agents and others, in such manner and to such amount as may be approved or directed by the Secretary of the Treasury.

SUPERVISING SPECIAL AGENTS TO RENDER MONTHLY ACCOUNT CURRENT.

XVII. Each Supervising Special Agent or other person, as afore-said, shall make a full record of each lot or parcel of property com-ing to his possession, in the manner prescribed by Regulation IV, and report the same, and all sales or other disposition thereof, made by him, rendering a monthly account current of all his transactions to the Secretary, accompanying the same with receipts or other vouchers for all moneys paid out by him. All balances remaining in his hands shall be deposited in the Treasury, from time to time, as directed by the Secretary.

ABANDONED AND CONFISCABLE LANDS, HOUSES, AND TENEMENTS.

REGULATIONS

CONCERNING THE CHARGE AND LEASING OF ABANDONED AND CONFISCABLE LANDS, HOUSES AND TENEMENTS, IN STATES DECLARED IN INSURRECTION, MADE IN PURSUANCE OF THE ACT OF CONGRESS ON THAT SUBJECT, AP-PROVED JULY 2. 1864.

Agents to carry out these Regulations.

I. The Regulations relative to abandoned and confiscable lands, houses and tenements will be carried into effect by the same Agents, and under the same supervision as are provided under the Regulations concerning commercial intercourse.

Agents to take Possession of Abandoned Lands, Tenements, &c.

II. The Supervising Special Agent of each Agency, and such Assistant Special Agents therein, as shall be designated for that purpose, will take possession of all lands, houses and tenements therein, abandoned by the lawful owners thereof, and all such as are confiscable under the act of Congress approved July 17, 1862.

Assistant Agent to keep Record and make Report.

III. When an Assistant Special Agent shall take possession of any such property, he will promptly record in a book to be kept by him for that purpose, a full description of the property, with a statement of its condition, the name of the owner, and any facts relating to him, or to the property which may affect the rights of the United States or of others interested in the property, one copy of which record he will promptly transmit to the Secretary of the Treasury, and one copy to the proper Supervising Special Agent, who will record the same in a book to be kept for that purpose.

Supervising Special Agent make Record and Report.

IV. When a Supervising Special Agent shall take possession of any such property, he will make a record as above required of an

Assistant Special Agent, and will transmit a copy thereof to the Secretary of the Treasury.

Lands, Tenements, &c., to be Leased.

V. All property so possessed will be rented as soon as practicable by the Supervising Special Agent or the Assistant Special Agent, under his direction, having such possession. No lease will be made for more than twelve months, and, when practicable, such property shall be rented from month to month. All leases will be in writing, and those for Plantations shall be in the following form:

Memorandum of an Agreement made this .... day of .... 186 ′ between .... Special Agent of the Treasury Department duly appointed under the Acts of Congress respectively approved March 12, 1863, and July 2, 1864, for taking charge of captured and abandoned property, and leasing abandoned and confiscable lands, houses, and tenements in the .... Agency, and........................of .... in the County of .... and State of ....

Witnesseth, that in pursuance of said Acts, and of the instructions of the Secretary of the Treasury, the said Agent, for and in behalf of the United States, agrees, upon the terms hereinafter contained, to lease to the said .... from the .... day of .... 186... to the .... day of .... 186... the following described lands and premises, to wit: ....

And the said .... hereby agrees that one equal .... part of the productions realized by the cultivation and working of the plantation aforesaid shall be promptly gathered, prepared and delivered to the authorized Agent of the United States at .... on or before the .... day of .... 186... in proper packages and condition for transportation.

And the said .... further agrees in relation to the employment and payment of freedmen worked upon the said plantation, that he will employ and pay them, and provide for their families in compliance with the Regulations of the Secretary of the Treasury, dated July 29, 1864, concerning the employment and general welfare of freedmen, which Regulations are made a part of this agreement so far as they relate to employers and employed, and further that he will do all things required of him by the Regulations of the Secretary of the Treasury concerning abandoned, captured, and confiscable property.

Signed, sealed and delivered ⎫
  in presence of   ⎭

—— ——, [L. S.]
—— ——, [L. S.]

When Lease is for Houses and Tenements only.

VI. When the lease is for houses and tenements only, then it shall be in the above form to the words "to lease to the said ------------," and instead of what follows therein insert as follows:

from the .... day of ...., 18......, from month to month, either party hereto being at liberty to terminate this lease at the end of any month from the date hereof, the following described premises: ....

And the said .... hereby agrees to pay the said Agent .... dollars per month, for each month from the date hereof, so long as he shall continue in possession of the said premises, and to pay the rent of each month in advance, and at the expiration of this lease as aforesaid to deliver possession of the said property to the said Agent, or his successor, in as good condition as the same is now in; loss by fire or other unavoidable injury excepted.

Signed, sealed and delivered ⎱
in presence of— ⎰

————— —————, [L. S.]
————— —————, [L. S.]

Leases to be made in triplicate.

VII. All leases of lands, houses, and tenements shall be made in triplicate, one of which shall be retained by the lessee, one will be retained by the Special Agent making the lease, and one will be forwarded to the Secretary of the Treasury. A record will be made by each agent making a lease, containing a copy thereof, and any facts connected therewith which may affect the same. A copy of the record will also be made in a book kept by the Supervising Special Agent for that purpose.

Agent to Receipt for Rents.

VIII. Upon the receipt of products or money for rent, the Agent receiving the same will indorse his receipt therefor upon the copy of the lease held by the lessee, and also give him a certified copy of the receipt, which the lessee will promptly forward to the Secretary of the Treasury.

Assistant Agents to keep Record of Rents received.

IX. When products or money shall be received by an Assistant Special Agent, he will make an entry in his books of account, stating the products or amount of money so received, the name of the person from whom received, and the lease upon account of which they are paid, the date of receipt, and any other facts connected therewith which should be recorded. He will promptly send the products or money so received, with a copy of the entry made, to the proper Supervising Special Agent, who will credit the products or money in his books of account, and make an entry in each case similar to that above required, and send duplicate receipts in each case to the Assistant Special Agent, who will retain one copy and send the other to the Secretary of the Treasury.

Supervising Agents to keep Record of Rents received.

X. When the products or moneys are received by a Supervising Special Agent, he will make the same entry above required of Assistant Special Agents, in his books of account, and will send a copy thereof to the Secretary of the Treasury.

Description of Confiscable Lands, Tenements, &c., to be kept.

XI. A careful description of all lands, houses, and tenements taken possession of by a Supervising Special Agent, or by his direction, as confiscable, will be recorded by him in a book kept for that purpose, in which will be entered all allegations against the owner which are relied on for condemnation, together with the names and residence of the witnesses to substantiate them, a copy of which record in each case will be sent to the Secretary of the Treasury.

Copy of Record of Confiscable Lands, &c., to be sent to United States District Attorney in certain cases.

XII. When any such lands, houses, and tenements are situated in a district within jurisdiction of a Federal Court exercising its functions, a copy of the above record, together with a statement of any other facts known to the Supervising Special Agent affecting the same, will be sent by him to the proper United States District Attorney, that proceedings for confiscation may be instituted, but such Agent will continue in charge of the property until relieved therefrom by order of the Court in which such proceedings are instituted.

Products Received for Rents to be Sold.

XIII. Supervising Special Agents will sell or dispose of all products received by them for rents, in the same manner and subject to the same Regulations as are prescribed by the Secretary of the Treasury concerning the sale and disposition of captured, abandoned, and confiscable personal property.

Money Received for Rents to be Deposited.

XIV. All money arising from rents, after payment therefrom of any expenses that may be approved by the Secretary of the Treasury, will be deposited by the Supervising Special Agents, with a designated United States Depository or Assistant Treasurer, and each Supervising Special Agent will make a full record of all his proceedings, and will report the same from time to time to the Secretary of the Treasury, and will render to him a monthly account current of all his transactions, accompanying the same with receipts or other vouchers for all moneys paid out by him, referring to the letter of approval thereof from the Secretary of the Treasury.

Employment and Welfare of Freedmen.

XV. In leasing abandoned and confiscable lands, provisions shall be made, as far as practicable, for the employment and general welfare of freedmen, and provision may be made in such leases, and also with those working their own lands and employing freedmen under rules established in relation thereto, for obtaining supplies free from the payment of the fee charged in other cases, and for the support of the helpless among such freedmen.

FREEDMEN.

REGULATIONS

PROVIDING FOR THE EMPLOYMENT AND GENERAL WELFARE OF ALL PERSONS WITHIN THE LINES OF NATIONAL MILITARY OCCUPATION WITHIN INSURRECTIONARY STATES, FORMERLY HELD AS SLAVES, WHO ARE OR SHALL BECOME FREE.

Agents to carry out these Regulations.

I. The Regulations relative to the employment and general welfare of freedmen will be carried into effect by the same Agents, and under the same supervision as are provided under the Regulations concerning commercial intercourse.

Freedmen's Home Colonies.

II. There shall be established in each Special Agency one or more places to be known as "Freedmen's Home Colonies," where all freed persons within the Agency may be received and provided for in pursuance of these Regulations.

Superintendent of Freedmen—His Duties.

III. A Superintendent of Freedmen will be appointed for each one of these Colonies, under the general direction of the proper Supervising Special Agent. Superintendents will make such arrangements as shall be necessary at each Colony to provide temporary shelter and care for persons received there, and also such buildings as are proper for the permanent use of those retained there; and will obtain such working animals and other agricultural implements of labor and other supplies as may be necessary and proper for the economical conduct of these establishments. They will also keep books of record in which shall be entered the name, age, condition, former owner, residence, and occupation of each person received in these Colonies; also, the marriages, births, and deaths occurring therein; also, all departures, and by whom those departing are employed, for what purpose, at what place, and on what terms.

Classification of Freedmen and their Wages.

IV. All persons of proper age and condition to labor, when received, shall be classified by the Superintendent as follows: Sound persons, over 18 and under 40 years of age, shall be classed as No. 1 hands; over 14 and under 18, and over 40 and under 55, No. 2; over 12 and under 14, and over 55, No. 3. Persons suffering from any physical defect or infirmity, but able to work, shall be classed as he considers proper. The minimum rate of wages of No. 1 males shall be $25 per month; No. 2, $20; No. 3, $15. Nos. 1, 2, and 3 females, $18, $14, $10. These rates shall not restrict mechanics and others from contracting for higher wages if they can do so.

Employment to be Provided for Freedmen of Proper Age.

V. Superintendents will see that all persons so received, registered, and classified, who are able to labor, are promptly provided with employment by lessees or others desiring their labor, upon the terms specified, and they will permit none over the age of twelve capable of labor to remain in idleness; and they will, as far as possible, obtain from planters and others the names and other particulars above specified, of all freed persons in their employ or within their knowledge in the district within which these Colonies are located, a record of which shall be kept by them as above provided, and they will do what they consistently can to see that all such persons are provided with employment at rates equal to those above specified, and that the helpless among them are properly cared for.

Applications for Laborers to be Received and Recorded.

VI. Superintendents will receive and record all applications for the labor of freedmen, that those received may be promptly furnished with employment. Planters and others employing parents will be required to take their children with them, unless the parent prefers to have them remain, in which case superintendents will see that provision is made to apply sufficient of the wages of the parent to support the children at the Colony.

Written Agreements to Le made between Employers and Employes, and Conditions.

VII. Superintendents shall see that written agreements are made between the employer and the employé, by which, in addition to the wages above fixed, the employer shall agree to furnish, without charge, sufficient quarters for the laborers, a separate tenement for each family, with proper regard for sanitary condition, one acre of ground for garden purposes to each family, fuel, medical attendance, and schools for children; also, that laborers shall be paid for full time, unless they are sick or voluntarily neglect to work; that one-half their monthly wages shall be paid to the laborer during each month, and the other half at the end of the term of employment; that, in case the laborer violates his contract by voluntary absence or continued neglect to work, the half wages due to him shall be forfeited, one half to the employer, and one half to the Government to aid in supporting the helpless; that any wages due to the laborers, under the agreement, shall be a first lien upon all crops produced, and that no shipment of products shall be made until the Superintendent shall certify that all dues to laborers are paid or satisfactorily arranged; that no labor in excess of ten hours per day shall be required, but if more shall be performed at the request of the employer extra payment shall be made therefor; that the employers shall keep on hand and sell to their employés, at actual cost on the plantation, a sufficient supply of wholesome food and proper clothing for themselves and their families.

Interest in Profits of Labor may be given instead of Wages.

VIII. In case any person employing Freedmen to labor on plantations shall wish to give an interest in the profits of their labor instead of the wages above fixed, and the laborers desire to accept the same, an agreement in writing may be made accordingly, subject to the approval of the proper Superintendent.

Where civil courts are established within reach of parties complaining under these agreements, they may seek redress there; but if no such courts are within reach, then the complaining party may state his case to a Superintendent, who, after hearing both parties, shall decide between them. Either party may appeal to the proper Supervising Special Agent, whose decision shall be final.

Care of Aged and Infirm Freedmen.

IX. Aged or infirm Freed persons, and orphan children under twelve years of age, and others unfit for regular labor who cannot be otherwise provided for, will be retained and provided for by Superintendents, and each Superintendent will see that all such persons under his care perform all such labor as is proper, considering their condition; and he will employ as many hands, at regular rates, as may be requisite for produce on the plantation all things that can be raised, necessary to the support of the establishment, and no more; and he will require all freed persons temporarily there to labor without wages, until they can be employed elsewhere. He will provide such medical attendance and schools as are necessary and proper.

Home Colonies may be Assigned to Associations upon certain Conditions.

X. Any Association or combination of Associations desiring to improve the condition of Freedmen, will have assigned to their care and general charge such Freedmen's Home Colonies as they may desire, and as they can give satisfactory assurance of their ability to provide for. Superintendents for any such colonies will be appointed upon the nomination and in pursuance of the wishes of such Associations, and every proper facility for the execution of their purposes will be given by the Supervising and Assistant Special Agents. Associations, desiring to operate under this clause, are notified that the Secretary reserves the right to revoke or modify this regulation whenever, in his judgment, the public interests will be promoted by such action.

Reservations of Land for Freedmen's Labor Colonies.

XI. For the purpose of promoting habits of industry and self-reliance among Freedmen, and to encourage them to locate in Colonies, and to enable them to work advantageously, there will be reserved in the respective Special Agencies such contiguous, abandoned, and confiscable lands and plantations as may be proper for that purpose, for the exclusive use and cultivation of Freedmen. which reservations will be called Freedmen's Labor Colonies. Over each of these Colonies there will be appointed a Superintendent for leasing small tracts therein to such Freedmen as are able to work them; and such lessees shall be subject to the same conditions and entitled to the same rights and privileges as other lessees.

Labor Colonies may be assigned to Associations on certain Conditions.

XII. Any Associatio,n or combination of Associations, desiring to aid lessees in such Colonies who have not sufficient means to cultivate without aid, will have set apart to their beneficiaries such part or the whole of any one of these Colonies as they shall give satisfactory assurance of their ability to provide for; and in case they agree to provide the necessary working animals, agricultural implements, seeds, and other aid which may be necessary for the cultivation of the whole of any such Colony, such Superintendent will be appointed as may be desired by the Association. Associations desiring to operate under this clause are notified, that the Secretary reserves the right to revoke or modify this Regulation whenever, in his judgment, the public interests will be promoted by such action.

Schools will be Established.

XIII. Schools will be established within these Home and Labor Colonies sufficient for the education of all children there under the age of twelve years, teachers for which will be provided by the Superintendent or by the Association, as the case may be.

Penalties for Ill Usage of Freedmen.

XIV. Ill usage of Freedmen by lessees or others employed by them, will be regarded as sufficient ground for the forfeiture of the contract between lessee and laborer, or, if the case be an aggravated one, of the lease of a plantation. Superintendents wi'l promptly and fully investigate complaints of this character, and if they prove to be well-founded, they will annul the contract for labor as above.

If, in their opinion, this action is inadequate, they will report the case to the proper Supervising Special Agent, who may, if he thinks proper, cancel the lease, subject to appeal to the General Agent.

Expenses to be approved by Secretary—Copies of all Papers to be Transmitted.

XV. All expenses must be authorized and approved by the Secretary of the Treasury. Each Superintendent, on the first of every month, will furnish the Secretary of the Treasury and the proper Supervising Special Agent with copies of all records, agreements, and other papers under his charge, and also a monthly statement of accounts, of all receipts and expenditures, with vouchers for all money paid out. Supervising Special Agents will render a monthly account current of all receipts and expenditures within their respective Agencies under these Regulations, accompanied with vouchers for all money paid by them.

ORDER OF SECRETARY OF WAR.

[General Orders No. 88.]

WAR DEPARTMENT,
WASHINGTON, *March* 31, 1863.

For the purpose of more effectually preventing all commercial intercourse with insurrectionary States, except such as shall be authorized in pursuance of law, and of securing consistent, uniform, and efficient action in conducting such intercourse as shall be so authorized, and for the purpose of carrying out the provisions of an act of Congress entitled "An act to provide for the collection of abandoned property and for the prevention of frauds in insurrectionary States," approved March 12, 1863, it is hereby ordered—

I.

That no officer of the army of the United States, nor other person connected therewith, shall authorize or have any interest in the transportation of any goods, wares, or merchandise (except supplies belonging to or contracted for by the United States, designed for the military or naval forces thereof, and moving under military or naval orders, and except, also, sutlers' supplies and other things necessary for the use and comfort of the troops of the United States, and moving under permits of the authorized officers of the Treasury Department) into any State declared by the President to be in insurrection; nor authorize nor have any interest in the purchase or sale therein of any goods or chattels, wares or merchandise, cotton, tobacco, or other product of the soil thereof; nor the transportation of the same, except as aforesaid, therefrom or therein; nor shall any such officer or person authorize, prohibit, or in any manner interfere with any such purchase or sale or transportation, which shall be conducted under the regulations of the Secretary of the Treasury, unless under some imperative military necessity, in the place or section where the same shall be conducted, or unless requested by an agent or some other authorized officer of the Treasury Department, in which case all commanders of military departments, districts, and posts, will render such aid in carrying out the provisions of the said act, and in enforcing due observance of the said regulations of the

4

Secretary of the Treasury, as can be given without manifest injury to the public service.

II.

It is further ordered that every officer or private, or person employed in or with the regular or volunteer forces of the United States, who may receive or have under his control any property which shall have been abandoned by the owner or owners, or captured in any district declared to be in insurrection against the United States, including all property seized under military orders, excepting only such as shall be required for military use of the United States forces, shall promptly turn over all such property to the agent appointed by the Secretary of the Treasury to receive the same, who shall give duplicate receipts therefor.

And every such officer or private, or person employed in or with the regular or volunteer forces of the United States, shall also promptly turn over to such agent, in like manner, all receipts, bills of lading, and other papers, documents, and vouchers showing title to such property, or the right to the possession, control, or direction thereof; and he shall make such order, indorsement, or writing as he has power to make, to enable such agent to take possession of such property or the proceeds thereof. Arms, munitions of war, forage, horses, mules, wagons, beef cattle, and supplies which are necessary in military operations, shall be turned over to the proper officers of the ordnance, or of the quartermaster, or of the commissary departments, respectively, for the use of the army. All other property abandoned or captured or seized, as aforesaid, shall be delivered to the agent appointed by the Secretary of the Treasury.

The officer receiving or turning over such property shall give the usual and necessary invoices, receipts, or vouchers therefor, and shall make regular returns thereof, as prescribed by the Army Regulations. The receipts of the agents of the Treasury Department shall be vouchers for all property delivered to them, and whenever called upon by the agent of the Treasury Department authorized to receive such abandoned or captured or seized property, as aforesaid, or the proceeds thereof, all persons employed in the military service will give him full information in regard thereto; and if requested by him so to do, they shall give him duplicates or copies of the reports and returns thereof, and of the receipts, invoices, and vouchers therefor.

And every officer of the army of the United States, hereafter receiving abandoned or captured or seized property, or the proceeds thereof, or under whose order it may be applied to the use of the military forces, as aforesaid, shall, upon request of a duly authorized agent of the Treasury Department, render a written report, with invoices thereof, to said agent, in which he will specify the arms, supplies, or other munitions of war, retained for the use of the military forces, as aforesaid, and also, separately, the property turned over to said agent, or which may have been sold or otherwise disposed of.

And in case a sale of any such property shall be made under his authority, or under the authority of any one subject to his order, he will so state, and will describe the property so sold, and will state when and where and by and to whom sold, and the amount received therefor, and what disposition was made of the proceeds.

And all officers of the army of the United States, will at all times render to the agents appointed by the Secretary of the Treasury all such aid as may be necessary to enable them to take possession of and transport all such property, so far as can be done without manifest injury to the public service.

III.

All commanders of military departments, districts, and posts, will, upon receipt of this order, revoke all existing orders within their respective commands conflicting or inconsistent herewith, or which permit or prohibit or in any manner interfere with any trade or transportation conducted under the regulations of the Secretary of the Treasury; and their attention is particularly directed to said regulations, prescribed March 31, 1863, and they will respectively make such orders as will insure strict observance of this order throughout their respective commands.

All expenses of transporting property herein referred to will be reported by the officers of the quartermaster's department, who furnish such transportation, to the agents of the Treasury Department, and also, through the ordinary channels, to the Quartermaster General at Washington, in order that the said expenses may be reimbursed from the proceeds of sales of such transported property.

EDWIN M. STANTON,
Secretary of War.

WAR DEPARTMENT,
July 29, 1864.

The attention of all officers and soldiers of the army of the United States, whether volunteer or regular, is specially directed to the regulations of the Secretary of the Treasury, approved by President, dated July 29, 1864, and superseding the regulations of September 11, 1863; and they will in all respects observe General Order of this Department numbered eighty-eight, and dated March 31, 1863, with regard to said Regulations of July 29, 1864, as if the same had been originally framed and promulgated with reference to them; and attention is called to the several acts of Congress appended hereto and especially to sections nine and ten of the act approved July 2, 1864.

EDWIN M. STANTON,
Secretary of War.

ORDER OF SECRETARY OF NAVY.

NAVY DEPARTMENT,
WASHINGTON, *March* 31, 1863.

For the purpose of more effectually preventing all commercial intercourse with insurrectionary States, except such as shall be authorized in pursuance of law, and of securing consistent, uniform, and efficient action in conducting such intercourse as shall be so authorized, and for the purpose of carrying out the provisions of an act of Congress entitled "An act to provide for the collection of abandoned property and for the prevention of frauds in insurrectionary States," approved March 12, 1863, it is hereby ordered—

I.

That no officer of the navy of the United States, nor other person connected therewith shall authorize or have any interest in the transportation of any goods, wares, or merchandise (except supplies belonging to or contracted for by the United States, designed for the military or naval forces thereof, and moving under military or naval orders, and except also sutlers' supplies and other things necessary for the use and comfort of the naval forces of the United States, and moving under permits of the authorized officers of the Treasury Department) into any State declared by the President to be in insurrection ; nor authorize nor have any interest in the purchase or sale therein of any goods or chattels, wares or merchandise, cotton, tobacco, or other products of the soil thereof; nor the transportation of the same, except as aforesaid, therefrom or therein; nor shall any such officer or person authorize, prohibit, or in any manner interfere with any such purchase or sale or transportation which shall be conducted under the regulations of the Secretary of the Treasury, unless under some imperative military necessity in the place or section where the same shall be conducted, or unless requested by an agent or some other authorized officer of the Treasury Department, in which case all officers of the navy of the United States and other persons connected therewith will render such aid in carrying out the provisions of the said act and of the law, and in enforcing due observance of the said regulations of the Secretary of the Treasury as can be given without manifest injury to the public service.

II.

It is further ordered that every officer, sailor, or marine in the naval service of the United States who shall receive or have under his control any property which shall have been abandoned by the owner or owners, or captured in any district declared to be in insurrection against the United States, including all property seized in any such district, under naval orders, excepting only such as shall be required for the use of the naval forces of the United States, and as is excluded by the act of March 12, 1863, shall promptly turn over all such property to the agent appointed by the Secretary of the Treasury, to receive the same, who shall give receipts therefor, if desired.

And every such officer, sailor, or marine shall also turn over to such agent in like manner all receipts, bills of lading, and other papers, documents, and vouchers showing title to such property, or the right to the possession, control, or direction thereof; and he shall make such order, indorsement, or writing as he has power to make to enable such agent to take possession of such property, or the proceeds thereof. Arms, munitions of war, forage, horses, mules, wagons, beef cattle, and supplies which are necessary in naval operations, shall be turned over to the proper officers for the use of the navy. All other property abandoned, captured, or seized, as aforesaid, shall be delivered to the said agent of the Treasury Department.

The officer receiving or turning over such property shall give the usual and necessary invoices, receipts or vouchers therefor, and shall make regular returns thereof as prescribed by the Navy Regulations. The receipts of the agents of the Treasury Department shall be vouchers for all property delivered to them. And whenever called upon by the said agent of the Treasury Department authorized to receive such abandoned, or captured, or seized property, as aforesaid, or the proceeds thereof, all persons employed in the naval service of the United States will give him full information in regard thereto, and if requested by him so to do, they shall give him duplicates or copies of the reports and returns thereof, and of the receipts, invoices, and vouchers therefor.

And every officer of the navy of the United States hereafter receiving abandoned, or captured, or seized property in any insurrectionary State as aforesaid, or the proceeds thereof, or under whose order it may be applied to the use of the naval forces as aforesaid, shall, upon request of an agent appointed by the Secretary of the Treasury as aforesaid, render a written report, with invoices thereof, to said agent, in which he will specify the arms, supplies, or other munitions of war retained for use of the naval forces, as aforesaid, and also, separately, the property turned over to said agent, or which may have been sold or otherwise disposed of. And in case a sale of any such property shall be made under his authority, or under the authority of any one subject to his order, he will so state, and will describe the property so sold, and will state when and where, and by and to whom sold, and the amount received therefor, and what disposition was made of the proceeds.

And all officers of the navy of the United States will, at all times, render to the agents appointed by the Secretary of the Treasury all such aid as may be necessary to enable them to take possession of any abandoned, or captured, or seized property aforesaid, and in transporting the same, so far as can be done without manifest injury to the public service.

All expenses of transporting property herein referred to will be reported by the officers who furnish the transportation to the agent of the Treasury Department, and also, through the proper channels, to the Navy Department at Washington, in order that the expenses may be reimbursed from the proceeds of sales of such transported property.

III.

All naval officers in command of squadrons, vessels, or stations, . will, upon receipt of this order, revoke all existing orders throughout their respective commands conflicting or inconsistent herewith, or which permit, or prohibit, or in any manner interfere with any trade or transportation conducted under the regulations of the Secretary of the Treasury not understood as applying to any lawful maritime prize by the naval forces of the United States; and their attention is particularly directed to said regulations, prescribed March 31, 1863, and they will respectively make such orders as will insure strict observance of this order throughout their respective commands.

GIDEON WELLES,
Secretary of the Navy.

Navy Department,
July 29, 1864.

The attention of all officers, sailors and marines of the Navy of the United States is especially directed to the Regulations of the Secretary of the Treasury, approved by the President, dated July 29, 1864, and superseding the Regulations of September 13, 1863, and they will, in all respects, observe the order of this Department dated March 31, 1863, with regard to said Regulations of July 29, 1864, as if the same had been originally promulgated in reference to them; and attention is called to the several acts of Congress appended hereto, and especially to sections nine and ten of the said act approved July 2, 1864.

GIDEON WELLES,
Secretary of the Navy.

ORDER OF QUARTERMASTER GENERAL.

QUARTERMASTER GENERAL'S OFFICE,
WASHINGTON CITY, *August* 4, 1864.

[General Orders No. 32.]

I...All officers of the Quartermaster's Department, upon receiving from the duly authorized agents of the Treasury Department written application for the use of transportation by land or water for collecting and forwarding to market, abandoned, captured, and confiscable property, under the Regulations of the Secretary of the Treasury of 29th July, 1864, will submit such applications to their immediate commander, with such explanation as to the available means of transportation on hand, and the quantity called for by the application, as will enable the commanding officer to decide whether it can be furnished without interference with, or injury to the military service or operations of the troops under his command.

If approved by the commander, the transportation will be furnished.

II...Of all actual expenditures incurred by the Quartermaster's Department in executing this order, accurate account will be kept, which will be transmitted to the Quartermaster General, with full explanations, in order that the appropriation of the Quartermaster's Department may be reimbursed by the Treasury Department out of the proceeds of sales of property collected under this order.

No charge will be made for the use of steamers and sail vessels for the transportation or collection of such property, unless there is detention during the time of collecting, loading, or discharging the property.

For all time thus consumed the proper charges, as of time of chartered vessels, of crews, and for coal and stores consumed, will be made.

M. C. MEIGS,
Bvt. Maj. Gen. and Q. M. Gen.

PROCLAMATIONS OF THE PRESIDENT.

AUGUST 16, 1861.

BY THE PRESIDENT OF THE UNITED STATES OF AMERICA.

A PROCLAMATION.

Whereas, on the fifteenth day of April, eighteen hundred and sixty-one, the President of the United States, in view of an insurrection against the laws, Constitution, and Government of the United States, which had broken out within the States of South Carolina, Georgia, Alabama, Florida, Mississippi, Louisiana, and Texas, and in pursuance of the provisions of the act entitled "An act to provide for calling forth the militia to execute the laws of the Union, suppress insurrections, and repel invasions, and to repeal the act now in force for that purpose," approved February twenty-eight, seventeen hundred and ninety-five, did call forth the militia to suppress said insurrection, and to cause the laws of the Union to be duly executed, and the insurgents have failed to disperse by the time directed by the President; and whereas such insurrection has since broken out, and yet exists, within the States of Virginia, North Carolina, Tennessee, and Arkansas; and whereas the insurgents in all the said States claim to act under the authority thereof, and such claim is not disclaimed or repudiated by the persons exercising the functions of government in such State or States, or in the part or parts thereof in which such combinations exist, nor has such insurrection been suppressed by said States:

Now, therefore, I, ABRAHAM LINCOLN, President of the United States, in pursuance of an act of Congress approved July thirteen, eighteen hundred and sixty-one, do hereby declare that the inhabitants of the said States of Georgia, South Carolina, Virginia, North Carolina, Tennessee, Alabama, Louisiana, Texas, Arkansas, Mississippi, and Florida, (except the inhabitants of that part of the State of Virginia lying west of the Alleghany mountains, and of such other parts of that State and the other States hereinbefore named as may maintain a loyal adhesion to the Union and the Constitution, or may be, from time to time, occupied and controlled by forces of the United States engaged in the dispersion of said insurgents,) are in a state of insurrection against the United States, and that all commercial intercourse between the same and the inhabitants thereof, with the exceptions aforesaid, and the citizens of other States and other parts of the United States is unlawful, and will remain unlawful until such insurrection shall cease or has been suppressed; that all goods and chattels, wares and merchandise, coming from any of said States, with the exceptions aforesaid, into other parts of the United States, without the special license and permission of the President, through the Secretary of the Treasury, or proceeding to any of said States, with the exceptions aforesaid, by land or water, together with the vessel or vehicle conveying the same, or conveying persons to, or from said States, with said exceptions, will be forfeited to the United States; and that, from and after fifteen days from the issuing of this Proclamation, all ships and vessels belonging in whole or in part to any citizen or inhabitant of any of said States, with said exceptions, found at sea, or in any port of the United States, will be forfeited to the United States; and I hereby enjoin upon all district attorneys, marshals, and officers of the revenue and of the military and naval forces of the United States to be vigilant in the execution of said act, and in the enforcement of the penalties and forfeitures imposed or declared by it; leaving any party who may think himself aggrieved thereby to his application to the Secretary of the Treasury for the remission of any penalty or forfeiture, which the said Secretary is authorized by law to grant if, in his judgment, the special circumstances of any case shall require such remission.

In witness whereof I have hereunto set my hand, and caused the seal of the United States to be affixed.

Done at the City of Washington, this sixteenth day of August, in the year of our Lord eighteen hundred and sixty-one, and of the Independence of the United States of America the eighty-sixth.
[L. S.]

ABRAHAM LINCOLN.

By the President:
WILLIAM H. SEWARD, *Secretary of State.*

JULY 1, 1862.

BY THE PRESIDENT OF THE UNITED STATES.

A PROCLAMATION.

Whereas, in and by the second section of an act of Congress passed on the 7th day of June, A. D. 1862, entitled "An act for the collection of direct taxes in insurrectionary districts within the United States, and for other purposes," it is made the duty of the President to declare, on or before the first day of July then next following, by his proclamation, in what State and parts of States insurrection exists:

Now, therefore, be it known that I, ABRAHAM LINCOLN, President of the United States of America, do hereby declare and proclaim that the States of South Carolina, Florida, Georgia, Alabama, Louisiana, Texas, Mississippi, Arkansas, Tennessee, North Carolina, and the State of Virginia, except the following counties: Hancock, Brooke, Ohio, Marshal, Wetzel, Marion, Monongalia, Preston, Taylor, Pleasants, Tyler, Ritchie, Doddridge, Harrison, Wood, Jackson, Wirt, Roane, Calhoun, Gilmore, Barbour, Tucker, Lewis, Braxton, Upshur, Randolph, Mason, Putnam, Kanawha, Clay, Nicholas, Cabell, Wayne, Boon, Logan, Wyoming, Webster, Fayette, and Raleigh, are now in insurrection and rebellion, and by reason thereof the civil authorities of the United States is obstructed so that the provisions of the "Act to provide increased revenue from imports, to pay the interest on the public debt, and for other purposes," approved August fifth, eighteen hundred and sixty-one, cannot be peaceably executed, and that the taxes legally chargeable upon real estate under the act last aforesaid, lying within the States and parts of States as aforesaid, together with a penalty of fifty per centum of said taxes, shall be a lien upon the tracts or lots of the same, severally charged, till paid.

In witness whereof I have hereunto set my hand and caused the seal of the United States to be affixed.

Done in the city of Washington, this first day of July, in the year of [L. S.] our Lord one thousand eight hundred and sixty-two, and of the independence of the United States of America the eighty-sixth.

ABRAHAM LINCOLN.

By the President:

F. W. SEWARD, *Acting Secretary of State.*

MARCH 31, 1863.

BY THE PRESIDENT OF THE UNITED STATES OF AMERICA.

A PROCLAMATION.

Whereas, in pursuance of the act of Congress approved July 13, 1861, I did, by proclamation, dated August 16, 1861, declare that the inhabitants of the States of Georgia, South Carolina, Virginia, North Carolina, Tennessee, Alabama, Louisiana, Texas, Arkansas, Mississippi, and Florida (except the inhabitants of that part of Virginia lying west of the Alleghany mountains, and of such other parts of that State, and the other States hereinbefore named as might maintain a loyal adhesion to the Union and the Constitution, or might be from time to time occupied and controlled by forces of the United States engaged in the dispersion of said insurgents) were in a state of insurrection against the United States, and that all commercial intercourse between the same and the inhabitants thereof, with the exceptions aforesaid, and the citizens of other States and other parts of the United States, was unlawful, and would remain unlawful until such insurrection should cease or be suppressed, and that all goods and chattels, wares, and merchandise coming from any of said States, with the exceptions aforesaid, into other parts of the United States, without the license and permission of the President, through the Secretary of the Treasury, or proceeding to any of said States, with the exceptions aforesaid, by land or water, together with the vessel or vehicle conveying the same to or from said States, with the exceptions aforesaid, would be forfeited to the United States.

And whereas experience has shown that the exceptions made in and by said proclamation embarrass the due enforcement of said act of July 13, 1861, and the proper regulation of the commercial intercourse authorized by said act with the loyal citizens of said States :

Now, therefore, I, ABRAHAM LINCOLN, President of the United States, do hereby revoke the said exceptions, and declare that the inhabitants of the States of Georgia, South Carolina, North Carolina, Tennessee, Alabama, Louisiana, Texas, Arkansas, Mississippi, Florida, and Virginia (except the forty eight counties of Virginia designated as West Virginia, and except, also, the ports of New Orleans, Key West, Port Royal, and Beaufort, in North Carolina) are in a state of insurrection against the United States, and that all commercial intercourse, not licensed and conducted as provided in said act, between the said States and the inhabitants thereof, with the exceptions aforesaid, and the citizens of other States and other parts of the United States, is unlawful, and will remain unlawful until such insurrection shall cease or has been suppressed, and notice thereof has been duly given by proclamation ; and all cotton, tobacco, and other products, and all other goods and chattels, wares and merchandise coming from any of said States, with the exceptions aforesaid, into other parts of the United States, or proceeding to any of said States, with the exceptions aforesaid, without the license and permission of the President, through the Secretary of the Treasury, will, together with the vessel or vehicle conveying the same, be forfeited to the United States.

In witness whereof I have hereunto set my hand and caused the seal [L. S.] of the United States to be affixed. Done at the city of Washington, this thirty-first day of March, A. D. 1863, and of the independence of the United States of America the eighty-seventh.

ABRAHAM LINCOLN.

By the President :
    WILLIAM H. SEWARD,
        Secretary of State.

BY THE PRESIDENT OF THE UNITED STATES.

A PROCLAMATION.

Whereas, in and by the Constitution of the United States, it is provided that the President "shall have power to grant reprieves and pardons for offences against the United States, except in cases of impeachment;" and

Whereas a rebellion now exists whereby the loyal State governments of several States have for a long time been subverted, and many persons have committed and are now guilty of treason against the United States; and

Whereas, with reference to said rebellion and treason, laws have been enacted by Congress, declaring forfeitures and confiscation of property and liberation of slaves, all upon terms and conditions therein stated, and also declaring that the President was thereby authorized at any time thereafter, by proclamation, to extend to persons who may have participated in the existing rebellion, in any State or part thereof, pardon and amnesty, with such exceptions and at such times and on such conditions as he may deem expedient for the public welfare; and

Whereas the congressional declaration for limited and conditional pardon accords with well-established judicial exposition of the pardoning power; and

Whereas, with reference to said rebellion, the President of the United States has issued several proclamations, with provisions in regard to the liberation of slaves; and

Whereas it is now desired by some persons heretofore engaged in said rebellion to resume their allegiance to the United States, and to reinaugurate loyal State governments within and for their respective States:

Therefore, I, ABRAHAM LINCOLN, President of the United States, do proclaim, declare, and make known to all persons who have, directly or by implication, participated in the existing rebellion, except as hereinafter excepted, that a full pardon is hereby granted to them and each of them, with restoration of all rights of property, except as to slaves, and in property cases where rights of third parties shall have intervened, and upon the condition that every such person shall take and subscribe an oath, and thenceforward keep and maintain said oath inviolate; and which oath shall be registered for permanent preservation, and shall be of the tenor and effect following, to wit:

"I, ———— ————, do solemnly swear, in presence of Almighty God, that I will henceforth faithfully support, protect, and defend the Constitution of the United States, and the union of the States thereunder; and that I will, in like manner, abide by and faithfully support all acts of Congress passed during the existing rebellion with reference to slaves, so long and so far as not repealed, modified, or held void by Congress, or by decision of the Supreme Court; and that I will, in like manner, abide by and faithfully support all proclamations of the President made during the existing rebellion having reference to slaves, so long and so far as not modified or declared void by decision of the Supreme Court. So help me God."

The persons excepted from the benefits of the foregoing provisions are all who are, or shall have been, civil or diplomatic officers or agents of the so-called confederate government; all who have left judicial stations under the United States to aid the rebellion; all who are, or shall have been, military or naval officers of said so-called confederate government above the rank of colonel in the army, or of lieutenant in the navy; all who left seats in the United States Congress to aid the rebellion; all who resigned commissions in the army or navy of the United States, and afterwards aided the rebellion; and all who have engaged in any way in treating colored persons, or white persons in charge of such, otherwise than lawfully as prisoners of war, and which persons may have been found in the United States service as soldiers, seamen, or in any other capacity.

And I do further proclaim, declare, and make known, that whenever, in any of the States of Arkansas, Texas, Louisiana, Mississippi, Tennessee, Alabama, Georgia, Florida, South Carolina, and North Carolina, a number of persons, not less than one-tenth in number of the votes cast in such State at the Presidential election of the year of our Lord one thousand eight hundred and sixty, each having taken the oath aforesaid and not having since violated it, and being a qualified voter by the election law of the State existing immediately before the so-called act of secession, and excluding all others, shall re-establish a State government which shall be republican, and in nowise contravening said oath, such shall be recognized as the true government of the State, and the State shall receive thereunder the benefits of the constitutional provision which declares that " The United States shall guaranty to every State in this Union a republican form of government, and shall protect each of them against invasion; and, on application of the legislature, or the executive, (when the legislature cannot be convened,) against domestic violence."

And I do further proclaim, declare, and make known that any provision which may be adopted by such State government in relation to the freed people of such State, which shall recognize and declare their permanent freedom, provide for their education, and which may yet be consistent, as a temporary arrangement, with their present condition as a laboring, landless, and homeless class, will not be objected to by the national Executive. And it is suggested as not improper, that, in constructing a loyal State government in any State, the name of the State, the boundary, the subdivisions, the constitution, and the general code of laws, as before the rebellion, be maintained, subject only to the modifications made necessary by the conditions hereinbefore stated, and such others, if any, not contravening said conditions, and which may be deemed expedient by those framing the new State government.

To avoid misunderstanding, it may be proper to say that this proclamation, so far as it relates to State governments, has no reference to States where loyal State governments have all the while been maintained. And for the same reason, it may be proper to further say, that whether members sent to Congress from any State shall be admitted to seats constitutionally rests exclusively with the respective Houses, and not to any extent with the Executive. And still further, that this proclamation is intended to present the people of the States wherein the national authority has been suspended, and loyal State governments have been subverted, a mode in and by which the national authority and loyal State governments may be re-established within said States, or in any of them; and, while the mode presented is the best the Executive can suggest, with his present impressions, it must not be understood that no other possible mode would be acceptable.

Given under my hand at the City of Washington, the eighth day of December, [L. S.] A. D. one thousand eight hundred and sixty-three, and of the independence of the United States of America the eighty-eighth.

ABRAHAM LINCOLN.

By the President:
WILLIAM H. SEWARD, *Secretary of State.*

ACTS OF CONGRESS.

AN ACT,

Approved March 2, 1799,

To regulate the collection of duties on imports and tonnage, referred to in 5th section of the act approved May 20, 1862, and 4th section of the act approved March 12, 1863, appended hereto.

Sec 91. *And be it further enacted*, That all fines, penalties, and forfeitures recovered by virtue of this act (and not otherwise appropriated) shall, after deducting all proper costs and charges, be disposed of as follows : one moiety shall be for the use of the United States, and be paid into the Treasury thereof by the collector receiving the same; the other moiety shall be divided between, and paid in equal proportions to the collector and naval officer of the district and surveyor of the port wherein the same shall have been incurred, or to such of the said officers as there may be in the said district; and in districts where only one of the aforesaid officers shall have been established, the said moiety shall be given to such officer.

Provided, nevertheless, That in all cases where such penalties, fines, and forfeitures shall be recovered in pursuance of information given to such collector by any person other than the naval officer or surveyor of the district, the one half of such moiety shall be given to such informer, and the remainder thereof shall be disposed of between the collector, naval officer, and surveyor or surveyors, in manner aforesaid.

Provided, also, That where any fines, forfeitures, and penalties incurred by virtue of this act, are recovered in consequence of any information given by any officer of a revenue cutter, they shall, after deducting all proper costs and charges, be disposed of as follows : one fourth part shall be for the use of the United States, and paid into the Treasury thereof in manner as before directed; one fourth part for the officers of the customs, to be distributed as hereinbefore set forth; and the remainder thereof to the officers of such cutter, to be divided among them agreeably to their pay.

And provided, likewise, That whenever a seizure, condemnation, and sale of goods, wares, or merchandise shall take place within the United States, and the value thereof shall be less than two hundred and fifty dollars, that part of the forfeiture which accrues to the United States, or so much thereof as may be necessary, shall be applied to the payment of the cost of prosecution.

And be it further provided, That if any officer or other person entitled to a part or share of any of the fines, penalties, or forfeitures incurred in virtue of this act, shall be necessary as a witness on the trial for such

fine, penalty, or forfeiture, such officer or other person may be a witness
upon the said trial; but in such case he shall not receive, nor be entitled
to any part or share of the said fine, penalty, or forfeiture, and the part
or share to which he otherwise would have been entitled, shall revert to
the United States.

Approved March 2, 1799.

AN ACT,

APPROVED JULY 13, 1861,

Further to provide for the collection of duties on imports, and for other purposes.

*Be it enacted by the Senate and House of Representatives of the United
States of America in Congress assembled,* That whenever it shall, in the
judgment of the President, by reason of unlawful combinations of persons in opposition to the laws of the United States, become impracticable to execute the revenue laws and collect the duties on imports by
ordinary means, in the ordinary way, at any port of entry in any collection district, he is authorized to cause such duties to be collected at any
port of delivery in said district until such obstruction shall cease; and
in such case the surveyors at said ports of delivery shall be clothed with
all the powers and be subject to all the obligations of collectors at ports
of entry; and the Secretary of the Treasury, with the approbation of
the President, shall appoint such number of weighers, gaugers, measu-
rers, inspectors, appraisers, and clerks, as may be necessary, in his judgment, for the faithful execution of the revenue laws at said ports of
delivery, and shall fix and establish the limits within which such ports
of delivery are constituted ports of entry, as aforesaid; and all the provisions of law regulating the issue of marine papers, the coasting trade,
the warehousing of imports, and collection of duties, shall apply to the
ports of entry so constituted in the same manner as they do to ports of
entry established by the laws now in force.

SEC. 2. *And be it further enacted,* That if, from the cause mentioned
in the foregoing section, in the judgment of the President, the revenue
from duties on imports cannot be effectually collected at any port of
entry in any collection district, in the ordinary way and by the ordinary
means, or by the course provided in the foregoing section, then and in
that case he may direct that the custom-house for the district be established in any secure place within said district, either on land or on board
any vessel in said district, or at sea near the coast; and in such case the
collector shall reside at such place, or on shipboard, as the case may be,
and there detain all vessels and cargoes arriving within or approaching
said district, until the duties imposed by law on said vessels and their
cargoes are paid in cash: *Provided,* That if the owner or consignee of
the cargo on board any vessel detained as aforesaid, or the master of
said vessel, shall desire to enter a port of entry in any other district of
the United States where no such obstructions to the execution of the
laws exist, the master of such vessel may be permitted so to change the
destination of the vessel and cargo in his manifest, whereupon the collector shall deliver him a written permit to proceed to the port so des-

ignated : *And provided further*, That the Secretary of the Treasury shall, with the approbation of the President, make proper regulations for the enforcement on shipboard of such provisions of the laws regulating the assessment and collection of duties as in his judgment may be necessary and practicable.

SEC. 3. *And be it further enacted,* That it shall be unlawful to take any vessel or cargo detained as aforesaid from the custody of the proper officers of the customs, unless by process of some court of the United States; and in case of any attempt otherwise to take such vessel or cargo by any force, or combination, or assemblage of persons, too great to be overcome by the officers of the customs, it shall and may be lawful for the President, or such person or persons as he shall have empowered for that purpose, to employ such part of the army or navy or militia of the United States, or such force of citizen volunteers as may be deemed necessary, for the purpose of preventing the removal of such vessel or cargo, and protecting the officers of the customs in retaining the custody thereof.

SEC. 4. *And be it further enacted,* That if, in the judgment of the President, from the cause mentioned in the first section of this act, the duties upon imports in any collection district cannot be effectually collected by the ordinary means and in the ordinary way, or in the mode and manner provided in the foregoing section of this act, then and in that case the President is hereby empowered to close the port or ports of entry in said district, and in such case give notice thereof by proclamation; and thereupon all right of importation, warehousing, and other privileges incident to ports of entry, shall cease and be discontinued at such port so closed, until opened by the order of the President on the cessation of such obstructions; and if, while said ports are so closed, any ship or vessel from beyond the United States, or having on board any articles subject to duties, shall enter or attempt to enter any such port, the same, together with its tackle, apparel, furniture, and cargo, shall be forfeited to the United States.

SEC. 5. *And be it further enacted,* That whenever the President, in pursuance of the provisions of the second section of the act entitled "An act to provide for calling forth the militia to execute the laws of the Union, suppress insurrections, and repel invasions, and to repeal the act now in force for that purpose," approved February twenty-eight, seventeen hundred and ninety-five, shall have called forth the militia to suppress combinations against the laws of the United States, and to cause the laws to be duly executed, and the insurgents shall have failed to disperse by the time directed by the President, and when said insurgents claim to act under the authority of any State or States, and such claim is not disclaimed or repudiated by the persons exercising the functions of government in such State or States, or in the part or parts thereof in which said combination exists, nor such insurrection suppressed by said State or States, then and in such case it may and shall be lawful for the President, by proclamation, to declare that the inhabitants of such State, or any section or part thereof, where such insurrection exists, are in a state of insurrection against the United States; and thereupon all commercial intercourse by and between the same and the citizens thereof

5

and the citizens of the rest of the United States shall cease and be unlawful so long as such condition of hostility shall continue; and all goods and chattels, wares and merchandise, coming from said State or section into the other parts of the United States, and all proceeding to such State or section by land or water, shall, together with the vessel or vehicle conveying the same, or conveying persons to or from such State or section, be forfeited to the United States: *Provided, however,* That the President may, in his discretion, license and permit commercial intercourse with any such part of said State or section, the inhabitants of which are so declared in a state of insurrection, in such articles, and for such time, and by such persons, as he, in his discretion, may think most conducive to the public interest; and such intercourse, so far as by him licensed, shall be conducted and carried on only in pursuance of rules and regulations prescribed by the Secretary of the Treasury. And the Secretary of the Treasury may appoint such officers, at places where officers of the customs are not now authorized by law, as may be needed to carry into effect such licenses, rules, and regulations; and officers of the customs and other officers shall receive for services under this section, and under said rules and regulations, such fees and compensation as are now allowed for similar service under other provisions of law.

SEC. 6. *And be it further enacted,* That from and after fifteen days after the issuing of the said proclamation, as provided in the last foregoing section of this act, any ship or vessel belonging in whole or in part to any citizen or inhabitant of said State or part of a State whose inhabitants are so declared in a state of insurrection, found at sea, or in any port of the rest of the United States, shall be forfeited to the United States.

SEC. 7. *And be it further enacted,* That, in the execution of the provisions of this act, and of the other laws of the United States providing for the collection of duties on imports and tonnage, it may and shall be lawful for the President, in addition to the revenue cutters in service, to employ in aid thereof such other suitable vessels as may, in his judgment, be required.

SEC. 8. *And be it further enacted,* That the forfeitures and penalties incurred by virtue of this act may be mitigated or remitted, in pursuance of the authority vested in the Secretary of the Treasury by the act entitled "An act providing for mitigating or remitting the forfeitures, penalties, and disabilities accruing in certain cases therein mentioned," approved March third, seventeen hundred and ninety-seven, or in cases where special circumstances may seem to require it, according to regulations to be prescribed by the Secretary of the Treasury.

SEC. 9. *And be it further enacted,* That proceedings on seizures for forfeitures under this act may be pursued in the courts of the United States in any district into which the property so seized may be taken and proceedings instituted; and such courts shall have and entertain as full jurisdiction over the same as if the seizure was made in that district.

Approved July 13, 1861.

AN ACT,

Approved May 20, 1862.

Supplementary to an act approved on the thirteenth July, eighteen hundred and sixty-one, entitled "An act to provide for the collection of duties on imports, and for other purposes."

Be it enacted by the Senate and House of Representatives of the United States of America in Congress assembled, That the Secretary of the Treasury, in addition to the powers conferred upon him by the act of the thirteenth July, eighteen hundred and sixty-one, be, and he is hereby authorized to refuse a clearance to any vessel or other vehicle laden with goods, wares, or merchandise, destined for a foreign or domestic port, whenever he shall have satisfactory reason to believe that such goods, wares, or merchandise, or any part thereof, whatever may be their ostensible destination, are intended for ports or places in possession or under control of insurgents against the United States; and if any vessel or other vehicle for which a clearance or permit shall have been refused by the Secretary of the Treasury, or by his order, as aforesaid, shall depart or attempt to depart for a foreign or domestic port without being duly cleared or permitted, such vessel or other vehicle, with her tackle, apparel, furniture, and cargo, shall be forfeited to the United States.

SEC. 2. *And be it further enacted,* That whenever a permit or clearance is granted for either a foreign or domestic port, it shall be lawful for the collector of the customs granting the same, if he shall deem it necessary, under the circumstances of the case, to require a bond to be executed by the master or the owner of the vessel, in a penalty equal to the value of the cargo, and with sureties to the satisfaction of such collector, that the said cargo shall be delivered at the destination for which it is cleared or permitted, and that no part thereof shall be used in affording aid or comfort to any person or parties in insurrection against the authority of the United States.

SEC. 3. *And be it further enacted,* That the Secretary of the Treasury be, and he is hereby, further empowered to prohibit and prevent the transportation in any vessel or upon any railroad, turnpike, or other road or means of transportation within the United States, of any goods, wares, or merchandise, of whatever character, and whatever may be the ostensible destination of the same, in all cases where there shall be satisfactory reasons to believe that such goods, wares, or merchandise are intended for any place in the possession or under the control of insurgents against the United States; or that there is imminent danger that such goods, wares, or merchandise will fall into the possession or under the control of such insurgents; and he is further authorized, in all cases where he shall deem it expedient so to do, to require reasonable security to be given that goods, wares, or merchandise shall not be transported to any place under insurrectionary control, and shall not, in any way, be used to give aid or comfort to such insurgents; and he may establish all such general or special regulations as may be necessary or proper to carry into effect the purposes of this act; and if any goods, wares, or merchandise shall be transported in violation of this act, or of any regulation of the Secretary of the Treasury, established in pursuance thereof, or if any attempt shall be made so to transport them, all goods, wares, or merchandise so transported or attempted to be transported shall be forfeited to the United States.

SEC. 4. *And be it further enacted*, That the proceedings for the penalties and forfeitures accruing under this act may be pursued, and the same may be mitigated or remitted by the Secretary of the Treasury in the modes prescribed by the eighth and ninth sections of the act of July thirteenth, eighteen hundred and sixty-one, to which this act is supplementary.

SEC. 5. *And be it further enacted*, That the proceeds of all penalties and forfeitures incurred under this act, or the act to which this is supplementary, shall be distributed in the manner provided by the ninety-first section of the act of March second, seventeen hundred and ninety-nine, entitled " An act to regulate the collection of duties on imports and tonnage."

Approved May 20, 1862.

AN ACT,

APPROVED JULY 17, 1862,

To suppress Insurrection, to punish Treason and Rebellion, to seize and confiscate the property of Rebels, and for other purposes.

Be it enacted by the Senate and House of Representatives of the United States of America in Congress assembled, That every person who shall hereafter commit the crime of treason against the United States, and shall be adjudged guilty thereof, shall suffer death, and all his slaves, if any, shall be declared and made free; or, at the discretion of the court, he shall be imprisoned for not less than five years and fined not less than ten thousand dollars, and all his slaves, if any, shall be declared and made free, said fine shall be levied and collected on any or all of the property, real and personal, excluding slaves, of which the said person so convicted was the owner at the time of committing the said crime, any sale or conveyance to the contrary notwithstanding.

SEC. 2. *And be it further enacted*, That if any person shall hereafter incite, set on foot, assist, or engage in any rebellion or insurrection against the authority of the United States, or the laws thereof, or shall give aid or comfort thereto, or shall engage in, or give aid and comfort to, any such existing rebellion or insurrection. and be convicted thereof, such person shall be punished by imprisonment for a period not exceeding ten years, or by a fine not exceeding ten thousand dollars, and by the liberation of all his slaves, if any he have; or by both of said punishments, at the discretion of the court.

SEC. 3. *And be it further enacted*, That every person guilty of either of the offences described in this act shall be forever incapable and disqualified to hold any office under the United States.

SEC. 4. *And be it further enacted*, That this act shall not be construed in any way to affect or alter the prosecution, conviction, or punishment of any person or persons guilty of treason against the United States before the passage of this act, unless such person is convicted under this act.

SEC. 5. *And be it further enacted*, That, to insure the speedy termination of the present rebellion, it shall be the duty of the President of the United States to cause the seizure of all the estate and property, money, stocks, credits, and effects of the persons hereinafter named in this section, and to apply and use the same and the proceeds thereof for the support of the army of the United States, that is to say:

First. Of any person hereafter acting as an officer of the army or navy of the rebels in arms against the government of the United States.

Secondly. Of any person hereafter acting as President, Vice-President, member of Congress, judge of any court, cabinet officer, foreign minister, commissioner or consul of the so-called confederate States of America.

Thirdly. Of any person acting as Governor of a State, member of a convention or legislature, or Judge of any court of any of the so-called Confederate States of America.

Fourthly. Of any person who, having held an office of honor, trust, or profit in the United States, shall hereafter hold an office in the so-called Confederate States of America.

Fifthly. Of any person hereafter holding an office or agency under the government of the so-called Confederate States of America, or under any of the several States of the said Confederacy, or the laws thereof, whether such office or agency be national, state, or municipal in its name or character: *Provided*, That the persons, thirdly, fourthly, and fifthly above described shall have accepted their appointment or election since the date of the pretended ordinance of secession of the State, or shall have taken an oath of allegiance to, or to support the constitution of the so-called Confederate States.

Sixthly. Of any person who, owning property in any loyal State or Territory of the United States, or in the District of Columbia, shall hereafter assist and give aid and comfort to such rebellion; and all sales, transfers, or conveyances of any such property shall be null and void; and it shall be a sufficient bar to any suit brought by such person for the possession or the use of such property, or any of it, to allege and prove that he is one of the persons described in this section.

SEC. 6. *And be it further enacted*, That if any person within any State or Territory of the United States, other than those named as aforesaid, after the passage of this act, being engaged in armed rebellion against the Government of the United States, or aiding or abetting such rebellion, shall not, within sixty days after public warning and proclamation duly given and made by the President of the United States, cease to aid, countenance, and abet such rebellion, and return to his allegiance to the United States, all the estate and property, moneys, stocks, and credits of such person shall be liable to seizure as aforesaid, and it shall be the duty of the President to seize and use them as aforesaid or the proceeds thereof. And all sales, transfers, or conveyances, of any such property after the expiration of the said sixty days from the date of such warning and proclamation shall be null and void; and it shall be a sufficient bar to any suit brought by such person for the possession or the use of such property, or any of it, to allege and prove that he is one of the persons described in this section.

SEC. 7. *And be it further enacted,* That to secure the condemnation and sale of any of such property, after the same shall have been seized, so that it may be made available for the purpose aforesaid, proceedings in rem shall be instituted in the name of the United States in any district court thereof, or in any territorial court, or in the United States district court for the District of Columbia, within which the property above described, or any part thereof, may be found, or into which the same, if movable, may first be brought, which proceedings shall conform as nearly as may be to proceedings in admiralty or revenue cases, and if said property, whether real or personal, shall be found to have belonged to a person engaged in rebellion, or who has given aid or comfort thereto, the same shall be condemned as enemies' property and become the property of the United States, and may be disposed of as the court shall decree and the proceeds thereof paid into the treasury of the United States for the purposes aforesaid.

SEC. 8. *And be it further enacted,* That the several courts aforesaid shall have power to make such orders, establish such forms of decree and sale, and direct such deeds and conveyances to be executed and delivered by the marshals thereof where real estate shall be the subject of sale, as shall fitly and efficiently effect the purposes of this act, and vest in the purchasers of such property good and valid titles thereto. And the said courts shall have power to allow such fees and charges of their officers as shall be reasonable and proper in the premises.

SEC. 9. *And be it further enacted,* That all slaves of persons who shall hereafter be engaged in rebellion against the Government of the United States, or who shall in any way give aid or comfort thereto, escaping from such persons and taking refuge within the lines of the army ; and all slaves captured from such persons or deserted by them and coming under the control of the Government of the United States; and all slaves of such persons found *on* [or] being within any place occupied by rebel forces and afterwards occupied by the forces of the United States, shall be deemed captives of war, and shall be forever free of their servitude, and not again held as slaves.

SEC. 10. *And be it further enacted,* That no slave escaping into any State, Territory, or the District of Columbia, from any other State, shall be delivered up, or in any way impeded or hindered of his liberty, except for crime, or some offence against the laws, unless the person claiming said fugitive shall first make oath that the person to whom the labor or service of such fugitive is alleged to be due is his lawful owner, and has not borne arms against the United States in the present rebellion, nor in any way given aid and comfort thereto; and no person engaged in the military or naval service of the United States shall, under any pretence whatever, assume to decide on the validity of the claim of any person to the service or labor of any other person, or surrender up any such person to the claimant, on pain of being dismissed from the service.

SEC. 11. *And be it further enacted,* That the President of the United States is authorized to employ as many persons of African descent as he may deem necessary and proper for the suppression of this rebellion, and for this purpose he may organize and use them in such manner as he may judge best for the public welfare.

SEC. 12. *And be it further enacted*, That the President of the United States is hereby authorized to make provision for the transportation, colonization, and settlement, in some tropical country beyond the limits of the United States, of such persons of the African race, made free by the provisions of this act, as may be willing to emigrate, having first obtained the consent of the government of said country to their protection and settlement within the same, with all the rights and privileges of freemen.

SEC. 13. *And be it further enacted*, That the President is hereby authorized, at any time hereafter, by proclamation, to extend to persons who may have participated in the existing rebellion in any State or part thereof, pardon and amnesty, with such exceptions and at such time and on such conditions as he may deem expedient for the public welfare.

SEC. 14. *And be it further enacted*, That the courts of the United States shall have full power to institute proceedings, make orders and decrees, issue process, and do all other things necessary to carry this act into effect.

Approved July 17, 1862.

AN ACT,

APPROVED MARCH 12, 1863,

To provide for the collection of abandoned property and for the prevention of frauds in insurrectionary districts within the United States.

Be it enacted by the Senate and House of Representatives of the United States of America in Congress assembled, That it shall be lawful for the Secretary of the Treasury, from and after the passage of this act, as he shall from time to time see fit, to appoint a special agent or agents to receive and collect all abandoned or captured property in any State or Territory, or any portion of any State or Territory of the United States, designated as in insurrection against the lawful government of the United States by the proclamation of the President of July first, eighteen hundred and sixty-two: *Provided*, That such property shall not include any kind or description which has been used, or which was intended to be used, for waging or carrying on war against the United States, such as arms, ordnance, ships, steamboats, or other water craft, and the furniture, forage, military supplies, or munitions of war.

SEC. 2. *And be it further enacted*, That any part of the goods or property received or collected by such agent or agents may be appropriated to public use on due appraisement and certificate thereof, or forwarded to any place of sale within the loyal States as the public interests may require; and all sales of such property shall be at auction to the highest bidder, and the proceeds thereof shall be paid into the treasury of the United States.

SEC. 3. *And be it further enacted*, That the Secretary of the Treasury may require the special agents appointed under this act to give a bond with such securities and in such amount as he shall deem necessary, and to require the increase of said amounts, and the strengthening of said security, as circumstances may demand ; and he shall also cause a book or books of account to be kept, showing from whom such property was received, the cost of transportation, and the proceeds of the sale thereof. And any person claiming to have been the owner of any such abandoned or captured property may, at any time within two years after the suppression of the rebellion, prefer his claim to the proceeds thereof in the Court of Claims ; and on proof to the satisfaction of said court of his ownership of said property, of his right to the proceeds thereof, and that he has never given any aid or comfort to the present rebellion, to receive the residue of such proceeds, after the deduction of any purchase money which may have been paid, together with the expense of transportation and sale of said property, and any other lawful expenses attending the disposition thereof.

SEC. 4. *And be it further enacted*, That all property coming into any of the United States not declared in insurrection as aforesaid, from within any of the States declared in insurrection, through or by any other person than any agent duly appointed under the provisions of this act, or under a lawful clearance by the proper officer of the Treasury Department, shall be confiscated to the use of the Government of the United States. And the proceedings for the condemnation and sale of any such property shall be instituted and conducted under the direction of the Secretary of the Treasury, in the mode prescribed by the eighty-ninth and nineteenth sections of the act of March second, seventeen hundred and ninety-nine, entitled " An act to regulate the collection of duties on imports and tonnage." And any agent or agents, person or persons, by or through whom such property shall come within the lines of the United States unlawfully, as aforesaid, shall be judged guilty of a misdemeanor, and on conviction thereof shall be fined in any sum not exceeding one thousand dollars, or imprisonment for any time not exceeding one year, or both, at the discretion of the court. And the fines, penalties and forfeitures accruing under this act may be mitigated or remitted in the mode prescribed by the act of March three, seventeen hundred and ninety-seven, or in such manner, in special cases, as the Secretary of the Treasury may prescribe.

SEC. 5. *And be it further enacted*, That the fifth section of the " Act to further provide for the collection of the revenue upon the northern, northeastern, and northwestern frontier, and for other purposes," approved July fourteen, eighteen hundred and sixty-two, shall be so construed as to allow the temporary officers which had been or may be appointed at ports which have been or may be opened or established in States declared to be in insurrection by the proclamation of the President on the first of July, eighteen hundred and sixty-two, the same compensation which by law is allowed to permanent officers of the same position. or the ordinary compensation of special agents, as the Secretary of the Treasury may determine.

SEC. 6. *And be it further enacted*, That it shall be the duty of every officer or private of the regular or volunteer forces of the United States, or any officer, sailor. or marine in the naval service of the United States, upon the inland waters of the United States, who may take or receive any such abandoned property, or cotton, sugar, rice, or tobacco, from persons in such insurrectionary districts, or have it under his control, to turn the same over to an agent appointed as aforesaid, who shall give a receipt therefor ; and in case he shall refuse or neglect so to do, he shall be tried by a court-martial and shall be dismissed from the service, or, if an officer, reduced to the ranks, or suffer such other punishment as said court shall order, with the approval of the President of the United States.

SEC. 7. *And be it further enacted,* That none of the provisions of this act shall apply to any lawful maritime prize by the naval forces of the United States.

Approved March 12, 1863.

AN ACT,

APPROVED JULY 2, 1864,

In addition to the several acts concerning commercial intercourse between loyal and insurrectionary States, and to provide for the collection of captured and abandoned property, and the prevention of frauds in States declared in insurrection.

Be it enacted by the Senate and House of Representatives of the United States of America in Congress assembled, That sales of captured and abandoned property under the act approved March twelve, eighteen hundred and sixty-three, may be made at such places, in States declared in insurrection, as may be designated by the Secretary of the Treasury, as well as at other places now authorized by said act.

SEC. 2. *And be it further enacted,* That, in addition to the captured and abandoned property to be received, collected, and disposed of, as provided in said act, the said agents shall take charge of and lease, for periods not exceeding twelve months, the abandoned lands, houses, and tenements within the districts therein named, and shall also provide, in such leases or otherwise, for the employment and general welfare of all persons within the lines of national military occupation within said insurrectionary States formerly held as slaves, who are or shall become free.   Property, real or personal, shall be regarded as abandoned when the lawful owner thereof shall be voluntarily absent therefrom, and engaged, either in arms or otherwise, in aiding or encouraging the rebellion.

SEC. 3. *And be it further enacted,* That all moneys arising from the leasing of abandoned lands, houses, and tenements, or from sales of captured and abandoned property collected and sold in pursuance of said act or of this act, or from fees collected under the rules and regulations made by the Secretary of the Treasury, and approved by the President, dated respectively the twenty-eighth day of August, eighteen hundred and sixty-two, the thirty-first day of March, and the eleventh day of September, eighteen hundred and sixty-three, or under any amendments or modifications thereof, which have been or shall be made by the Secretary of the Treasury, and approved by the President, for conducting the commercial intercourse which has been or shall be licensed and per-

6

mitted by the President, with and in States declared in insurrection, shall, after satisfying therefrom all proper and necessary expenses to be approved by the Secretary of the Treasury, be paid into the treasury of the United States; and all accounts of moneys received or expended in connexion therewith shall be audited by the proper accounting officers of the treasury. That the first section of the "Act to provide for the collection of abandoned property and for the prevention of fraud in insurrectionary districts in the United States," approved March twelve, eighteen hundred and sixty-three, is hereby extended so as to include the descriptions of property mentioned in an act entitled "An act further to provide for the collection of duties on imports, and for other purposes," approved July thirteen, eighteen hundred and sixty-one, and an act entitled "An act to suppress insurrection, to punish treason and rebellion, to seize and confiscate the property of rebels, and for other purposes," approved July seventeen, eighteen hundred and sixty-two, respectively; and that the sales provided for in said act first mentioned may be made at such place as may be designated by the Secretary of the Treasury. And section six of said first-mentioned act is hereby amended so as to include every description of property mentioned in the acts of July thirteen, eighteen hundred and sixty-one, and July seventeen, eighteen hundred and sixty-two, aforesaid; and that all property, real or personal, described in the acts to which this is in addition, shall be regarded as abandoned when the lawful owner thereof shall be voluntarily absent therefrom, and engaged, either in arms or otherwise, in aiding or encouraging the rebellion.

SEC. 4. *And be it further enacted*, That the prohibitions and provisions of the act approved July thirteen, eighteen hundred and sixty-one, and of the acts amendatory or supplementary thereto, shall apply to all commercial intercourse by and between persons residing or being within districts within the present or future lines of national military occupation in the States or parts of States declared in insurrection, whether with each other or with persons residing or being within districts declared in insurrection and not within those lines; and that all persons within the United States, not native or naturalized citizens thereof, shall be subject to the same prohibitions, in all commercial intercourse with inhabitants of States or parts of States declared in insurrection, as citizens of loyal States are subject to under the said act or acts.

SEC. 5. *And be it further enacted*, That whenever any part of a loyal State shall be under the control of insurgents, or shall be in dangerous proximity to places under their control, all commercial intercourse therein and therewith shall be subject to the same prohibitions and conditions as are created by the said acts, as to such intercourse between loyal and insurrectionary States, for such time and to such extent as shall from time to time become necessary to protect the public interests, and be directed by the Secretary of the Treasury, with the approval of the President.

SEC. 6. *And be it further enacted*, That so much of the fifth section of the act approved May twenty, eighteen hundred and sixty-two, and the fourth section of the act approved March twelve, eighteen hundred and sixty-three, as directs the manner of distributing fines, penalties, and forfeitures, is hereby repealed, and that, in lieu of the distribution thereby directed to be made to informers, collectors, and other officers of the customs, the court decreeing condemnation may award such compensation to customs officers, informers, or other persons, for any service connected therewith, as will tend to promote vigilance in protecting the public interests, and as shall be just and equitable, in no case, however, to exceed the aggregate amount heretofore directed by the said fifth section.

SEC. 7. *And be it further enacted,* That no property seized or taken upon any of the inland waters of the United States by the naval forces thereof, shall be regarded as maritime prize ; but all property so seized or taken shall be promptly delivered to the proper officers of the courts, or as provided in this act and in the said act approved March twelve, eighteen hundred and sixty-three.

SEC. 8. *And be it further enacted,* That it shall be lawful for the Secretary of the Treasury, with the approval of the President, to authorize agents to purchase for the United States any products of States declared in insurrection, at such places therein as shall be designated by him, at such prices as shall be agreed on with the seller, not exceeding the market value thereof at the place of delivery, nor exceeding three-fourths of the market value thereof in the city of New York at the latest quotations known to the agent purchasing : *Provided,* That no part of the purchase money for any products so purchased shall be paid, or agreed to be paid, out of any other fund than that arising from property sold as captured or abandoned, or purchased and sold under the provisions of this act. All property so purchased shall be forwarded for sale at such place or places as shall be designated by the Secretary of the Treasury, and the moneys arising therefrom, after payment of the purchase money and the other expenses connected therewith, shall be paid into the treasury of the United States ; and the accounts of all moneys so received and paid shall be rendered to, and audited by, the proper accounting officers of the treasury.

SEC. 9. *And be it further enacted,* That so much of section five of the act of thirteenth of July, eighteen hundred and sixty-one, aforesaid, as authorizes the President, in his discretion, to license or permit commercial relations in any State or section the inhabitants of which are declared in a state of insurrection, is hereby repealed, except so far as may be necessary to authorize supplying the necessities of loyal persons residing in insurrectionary States, within the lines of actual occupation by the military forces of the United States, as indicated by published order of the commanding general of the department or district so occupied ; and, also, except so far as may be necessary to authorize persons residing within such lines to bring or send to market in the loyal States any products which they shall have produced with their own labor or the labor of freedmen or others employed and paid by them, pursuant to rules relating thereto, which may be established under proper authority. And no goods, wares, or merchandise shall be taken into a State declared in insurrection or transported therein, except to and from such places and to such monthly amounts as shall have been previously agreed upon in writing by the commanding general of the department in which such places are situated and an officer designated by the Secretary of the Treasury for that purpose.

SEC. 10. *And be it further enacted*, That all officers and privates of the regular and volunteer forces of the United States, and all officers, sailors, and marines in the naval service, are hereby prohibited from buying or selling, trading, or in any way dealing in the kind or description of property mentioned in this act, and the act to which this is in addition, whereby to receive or expect any profit, benefit, or advantage to himself or any other person, directly or indirectly connected with him. And it shall be the duty of such officer, private, sailor, or marine, when such property shall come into his possession or custody, or within his control, to give notice thereof to some agent appointed by virtue of this act, and to turn the same over to such agent without delay. Any officer of the United States, civil, military, or naval, or any sutler, soldier, marine, or other person, who shall violate any provision of this act, or who shall take or cause to be taken into a State declared to be in insurrection, or to any other point to be thence taken into such State, or who shall transport or sell, or otherwise dispose of therein, any goods, wares, or merchandise whatsoever, except in pursuance of license and authority of the President, as provided in said fifth section of the act of July thirteen, eighteen hundred and sixty-one, aforesaid, and any officer or other person aforesaid who shall make any false statement or representation upon which license and authority shall be granted for such transportation, sale, or other disposition, and any officer or other person aforesaid who shall, under any license or authority obtained, wilfully and knowingly transport, sell, or otherwise dispose of any other goods, wares, or merchandise than such as are in good faith so licensed and authorized, or shall wilfully and knowingly transport, sell, or dispose of the same, or any portion thereof, in violation of the terms of such license or authority, or of any rule or regulation prescribed by the Secretary of the Treasury concerning the same, or shall be guilty of any act of embezzlement, of wilful misappropriation of public or private money or property, of keeping false accounts, or of wilfully making any false returns, or of any other act amounting to a felony, shall be liable to indictment as for a misdemeanor, and fine not exceeding five thousand dollars, and to punishment in the penitentiary not exceeding three years, before any court, civil or military, competent to try the same. And it shall be the duty of the Secretary of the Treasury, from time to time, to institute such investigations as may be necessary to detect and prevent frauds and abuses in the trade and other transactions contemplated by this act or by the acts to which this is supplementary. And the agents making such investigations shall have power to compel the attendance of witnesses, and to make examinations on oath.

SEC. 11. *And be it further enacted*, That the Secretary of the Treasury, with the approval of the President, shall make such rules and regulations as are necessary to secure the proper and economical execution of the provisions of this act, and shall defray all expenses of such execution from the proceeds of fees imposed by said rules and regulations, of sales of captured and abandoned property, and of sales hereinbefore authorized.

Approved July 2, 1864.

www.ingramcontent.com/pod-product-compliance
Lightning Source LLC
Chambersburg PA
CBHW021524270326
41930CB00008B/1074